"Mitri Raheb's personal and moving chronicle of Bethlehem's siege reveals a little-known and rarely acknowledged human narrative of the Palestinian people's quest for dignity and freedom, even in the midst of devastation and pain. The struggle to endure and rebuild despite the Israeli occupation's persistent brutal assaults is a tribute to the unvanquished spirit of the 'ordinary' Palestinian. It is part of Raheb's passionate message to hold on to the spirit of resurrection and his insistence on seeing a beacon of hope where it is easy to see only darkness and despair."

—Hanan Ashrawi
Palestinian Rights Activist,
Founder, Palestinian Independent Commission for Citizen's Rights
Sydney Peace Prize recipient

"A pastor's home under military bombardment, his young daughters dodging machine-gun fire, elderly neighbors bleeding to death because ambulances are denied access—these are the painful and poignant images of war hidden behind the headlines of the Israeli siege of Bethlehem. Mitri Raheb's personal account replaces faceless statistics with traumatic stories of innocent persons caught in the crossfire of political hatred. With faith and hope, he challenges us to overcome our sins of indifference and insensitivity to the plight of the Palestinians and calls us to work for new relationships among Jews, Muslims, and Christians."

—Donald E. Messer
Henry White Warren Professor of Practical Theology and
President Emeritus, Iliff School of Theology, Denver, Colorado

"A powerful, first-person account . . . that brings the story alive, the fear as well as the hope. . . . Within the glimpses of life during these heart-stopping days, we see the seeds of hope for reconciliation that lie in faith, and in simple, helpful gestures that cross the lines of division. *Bethlehem Besieged* is a reminder that peace is always possible."

—Rev. Kent Winters-Hazelton
President, The Witherspoon Society, Presbyterian Church (USA)

"Bethlehem Besieged allows the readers to be a part of the community under siege in this most famous town. . . . It also tells powerful stories of healing and of rebuilding a sense of community in a place of deep brokenness. It is a story we can all learn from."

—Bernice Powell Jackson
Executive Minister, Justice and Witness Ministries,
United Church of Christ

"Once again, Rev. Mitri Raheb renders wise, poignant, and complex reflections about the plight of the Palestinians. This book is the living testimony of an Arab Palestinian Christian leader who has been helping to nurture . . . real promise of hope for a just peace in the Holy Land. *Bethlehem Besieged* is a book you must read. . . ."

—Rateb Y. Rabie
President, Holy Land Christian Ecumenical Foundation (HCEF)

"Bethlehem Besieged is first a document of horror and hope about the plight and possibilities that confront the Palestinian people. But it is also more. As a Jew I see this story as a warning to the Jewish people that we are becoming almost everything we loathed about our oppressors. For me, Mitri Raheb's gentle anger is a prophetic call to Jews in Israel and beyond to stop and reverse course before it is too late. . . . A gripping real-life story. . . ."

—Marc H. Ellis
Professor of American and Jewish Studies, Baylor University

"Mitri Raheb's book *Bethlehem Besieged* gives the readers a deep, although short, look into the lives of the Palestinian people. It shows the human dimensions of the Palestinian people, who are often dehumanized by the media. . . . This book is a message of peace."

—Mohammad Darawshe
Director of Public Relations, Givat Haviva Jewish Arab Center of
Peace and Co-Founder of OneVoice MidEast Peace Initiative

"This is not a resource to be picked up and read. Instead, it is an experience to be lived and shared with others! These are stories of health and hope, of Good Fridays and Easters, of worries, wars, and woes, with a few 'wows' thrown in. Mitri Raheb is a 'divine irritant' who must be heard and experienced. . . . "

—Rich Bimler
President, Wheat Ridge Ministries, Itasca, Illinois

BETHLEHEM BESIEGED

STORIES OF HOPE IN TIMES OF TROUBLE

Mitri Raheb

FORTRESS PRESS

MINNEAPOLIS

BETHLEHEM BESIEGED
Stories of Hope in Times of Trouble

Copyright © 2004 Augsburg Fortress. All rights reserved. Except for brief quotations in critical articles or reviews, no part of this book may be reproduced in any manner without prior written permission from the publisher. Write: Permissions, Augsburg Fortress, Box 1209, Minneapolis, MN 55440.

Scripture quotations from the New Revised Standard Version of the Bible are copyright © 1989 by the Division of Christian Education of the National Council of the Churches of Christ in the United States of America and are used by permission.

Cover photo: AP/Wide World Photos
Cover design: Kevin van der Leek
Interior design: James Korsmo
Paintings: Courtesy of the International Center of Bethlehem
Photographs: Musa al Shaer (pages 2, 26, 44, 70, 94, 110, 116, 142, 148) and Carina Appel (pages 34, 52)

Library of Congress Cataloging-in-Publication Data

Raheb, Mitri.
  Bethlehem besieged : stories of hope in times of trouble / Mitri Raheb.
    p. cm.
  ISBN 0-8006-3653-8 (alk. paper)
  1. Palestine in Christianity. 2. Arab-Israeli Conflit, 1993—Religious aspects—Christianity. 3. Raheb, Mitri. 4. Arab-Israeli Conflict, 1993—Personal narratives, Palestinian Arab. I. Title.
  BT93.8.R33 2004
  275.695'2083—dc22

                                                            2004008342

The paper used in this publication meets the minimum requirements of American National Standard for Information Sciences—Permanence of Paper for Printed Library Materials, ANSI Z329.48-1984.

Manufactured in the U.S.A.

Contents

To my daughters,
Dana (14) and Tala (10),
who were born, grew up, and might continue
to live in times of trouble, yet are sustained by the
Everlasting Hope

Preface

I am a Palestinian. For hundreds of years my family has lived and worked in Palestine. I am also a Christian, indeed a pastor in Bethlehem, birthplace of the Prince of Peace yet now strewn with the rubble of invasion and unrest. I am an Arab Christian, living in an Arab-Islamic context, a context very much shaped by an ongoing Israeli-Palestinian conflict.

I am not sure if it is my destiny to write books during difficult times. But writing in such a context becomes an act of nonviolent resistance: resisting being silenced, resisting being a spectator, and resisting giving up. Writing under siege overcomes the siege imposed on us, and publishing while the apartheid-like wall is being built enables me, in a sense, to transcend the wall. I was able to write this book under such circumstances only by the grace of God. It is grace if one is given a word to speak in times of trouble. It is grace if these words are not those of hate but of hope. It certainly is grace if these words can make a difference in the lives of those hearing and reading it in the little town of Bethlehem and around the world.

The turmoil in our country has been going on for so long that the biggest threat is for people to become indifferent—when watching events unfold people can "see and yet not see," when hearing breaking news people can "hear and yet not hear," thus leaving hearts untouched, closed, and cold. I write as a witness. In this little book, I ask you to witness too.

I would like to thank my wife, Najwa, as well as my colleagues Rana Khoury, Dr. Nuha Khoury, and Rev. Sandra Olewine, who took much of my workload and responsibilities, enabling me to have time to write. I owe special thanks to Beth Lewis, President of Augsburg Fortress, to Fortress Press Editor-in-Chief Michael West as well as to Ann Delgehausen, Bob Todd, and James Korsmo, for their commitment, enthusiasm, and professional service. Finally yet importantly, I would like to thank my colleagues at the International Center of Bethlehem as well as at the Dar al-Kalima Academy for helping me keep hope alive in the little town of Bethlehem, where hope sprang up 2000 years ago.

Under Siege

1

A Monk
at the Compound

It was 4:30 on Tuesday morning, April 2, 2002. The telephone rang at our home. We woke up scared. My wife asked me, "What's the matter? Who's calling so early in the morning?" I immediately thought it might be an emergency case in the congregation. Instead, the voice on the phone was my aunt who lives on the outskirts of Bethlehem: "Didn't you hear the news? The Israeli military is invading Bethlehem from five different directions!"

We'd expected the invasion. Israel had already invaded most of the Palestinian towns and villages. For the last two days, Israeli tanks had been gathering at the checkpoint leading to Bethlehem. But we hadn't expected such a massive operation. There was no reason to invade our "little town" with hundreds of military tanks and armored vehicles, accompanied by Apache helicopters. The excuse

Israel used for invading Bethlehem was a suicide bombing that took place on March 29 in Jerusalem by a young Palestinian woman from Deheishe refugee camp near Bethlehem. The blast killed Ayat al-Akhras and two Israeli people and injured two dozen more. The decision to invade, however, was made weeks before. Before the suicide bombing had taken place, Israeli Prime Minister Sharon had already launched his military offensive, called "Operation Defensive Shield," and Israeli forces were already rolling into Ramallah and had besieged Palestinian President Yasir Arafat in his headquarters. Three days later, they were in Bethlehem and in front of our house.

I looked out of the window. It was raining, and the wind was blowing. The sun had not yet risen, and the streets of Bethlehem were lit but empty. I saw no cars, no pedestrians, no movement whatsoever. In the background, I could hear a helicopter flying, but it was far from the Old City, where we live.

At 5:45 AM, we received another call from my aunt: "Israeli tanks have just passed our home. They are heading toward Bethlehem." I could hear the noise of the helicopter getting louder and louder. Clearly, the helicopter was following the tanks.

I turned on the lights and walked to our living room, where I turned on the TV and tuned to the local stations. They were broadcasting live coverage of the invasion, but without any pictures. It was impossible for any journalist to go outside and film anything. But every few minutes, the reporters would announce the movement of the Israeli tanks: Israeli Occupational Forces are approaching Bethlehem from the south, from the west, from the east, and from the north. Around 6:15 AM, the

TV screen announced that the Israeli Occupational Forces were heading toward the old town. They were entering Paul VI Street and moving toward Madbaseh Square.

I started rolling down all our window shutters. My wife was making the morning coffee. My mother, who lives next to the Nativity Church but had come to spend a few nights with us at our home, was holding her transistor radio, following the news as it unfolded.

We live in the parsonage within the Lutheran compound. To our west is Christmas Lutheran Church, to the east lies the International Center of Bethlehem, and to the south is Abu Gubran Guesthouse. West of Christmas Lutheran Church is Madbaseh Square. This old square marked the far west end of the city during the nineteenth century, but in the twentieth century it developed to become the heart of the city. From Madbaseh Square, two streets form a V leading to the Church of the Nativity, which is only three blocks away from our Christmas Lutheran Church. The Lutheran compound is like a triangle island within this V shape, bordered by the two main streets, Paul VI and Fawaghreh.

By this time, the Israeli tanks were already at Madbaseh Square. We could hear the tanks on both the north and south sides of our house. Everything was still calm, except for the helicopter, which by now was circling over our house. But this proved to be the calm before the storm. Around 6:30 AM, the fighting started. First we heard some shooting, *tac . . . tac . . . tac . . .* , and then we heard automatic machine guns, *tac tac tac tac tac tac.* Tanks were stationed on both sides of our compound.

The first thing I could think of was to protect our daughters. Dana, twelve years old, and Tala, eight, were still in their beds and asleep. Their bedroom has three large windows facing the west and the south, so bullets can easily enter, even with the shutters down. I asked my daughters to come to our sitting room, which has no outside windows, so it is one of the safest places in the house.

The shooting continued without much interruption. Every now and then, we heard something breaking or glass shattering. It was too dangerous to be close to any of the windows, so we had no idea what was going on. But from the sound, we could distinguish Palestinian guns firing one bullet at a time from the Israeli automatic machine guns firing their .50-caliber bullets in series. It seemed to me that some Palestinian gunmen were waiting for the Israeli troops in the Old Town. They knew they would have no chance to defend Bethlehem on the outskirts, but they might have a better chance in the Old Town. They might have calculated that the Israeli tanks couldn't enter the Old Town with its narrow roads and would therefore have to step out of the tanks and vehicles, giving the gunmen a chance to confront them on equal footing. We felt that we were caught in the middle. From the sounds, we could tell that the Israeli troops were on the west, south, and north sides of our compound, while the Palestinian gunmen were on the east side, in the direction of the Church of the Nativity.

The battle did not last long. After thirty minutes or so, we could no longer hear the Palestinian guns. We weren't sure what was happening. We wondered if the Israeli troops had killed the Palestinian gunmen. Or had they arrested the gunmen? What had happened? A text message on the TV screen said the gunmen were retreating toward the Church of the Nativity. The shooting stopped for a few minutes.

But then the firing broke out again. We didn't know quite why. We couldn't hear any more Palestinian gunmen shooting, but the gunfire was intensifying. It seemed that the Israeli soldiers had decided to heavily bombard the city center before storming it so they would ensure that no resistance would be left. Then the Israeli tank positioned outside our home entrance started firing. We could feel the whole house shaking. We could hear the long window facade of our main staircase at the southern end of the house blowing up. Little more than a single door was left between us and the streets. The noise of the Israeli guns and tanks was as loud and near as if they were inside the house.

The sitting room was no longer safe. We had to look for another room. We moved to my office and gathered in one corner very close to each other. The shooting was loud, and it was machine guns again. On the southern end, we heard another tank firing, then a big boom. Something had been destroyed. We could hear the destruction very clearly. It must have been very close to us. So this room also was not safe anymore. Every one of us was terrified. My mother was praying loudly. My wife was shaking. Tala, my younger daughter, was crying and clinging to me, while Dana was trying her best to comfort her grandmother.

We decided to move again to the other side of the house. We spent the next few hours running from one side of the house to the other. When the snipers and tanks in the northern end would fire, we would all run to the southern side, and vice versa. But occasionally both tanks would fire at the same time. "Oh, my God! Where should we go?" My daughters were crying, "Oh, Father, where should we go? What shall we do?" We decided to crawl along the floor and sit in the corridor behind the thickest concrete wall in the house. These were among the longest moments of our lives. We thought we would die or be buried alive under the ruins of our parsonage.

Thank God, after almost three uninterrupted hours, the shooting stopped. It was around 9:30 AM. We waited for about fifteen minutes and then moved back to our sitting room. The TV continued to broadcast the news. On the screen, we read that Israeli tanks had opened fire at Sami Abdeh's house, killing his brother Khalid (thirty-seven) and his mother Sumayya (sixty-four) in their home.

"These are our nextdoor neighbors!" my wife shouted.

"I know," I replied, thinking of old memories with Sami and his brothers, who had been students at our school. Khalid was a very shy person but loved Arabic language and history. Sami was a very bright student with excellent communication skills.

We continued watching the TV screen. The next text message read, "An Israeli tank fires at Lamas's house in Fawaghreh Street, opening a four-foot hole in their bedroom concrete wall."

"These are our neighbors on the other side!" I exclaimed. This newly married young Christian couple lived in the home across from our bedroom. We wondered if they had been hurt or even killed. But the television offered no more details. Instead, a new text message appeared, saying, "Israeli soldiers are preventing the ambulance from entering Paul VI Street to collect the dead bodies of Khalid Abdeh and his mother." And then we heard the voice of Sami, Khalid's brother, speaking in an anguished voice: "Israeli soldiers opened fire on my brother and my mother. Khalid died on the spot, and his head was immediately blown apart and distorted. My mother kept bleeding for hours. While holding her hands, I kept telling her not to be afraid, that the ambulance would come, that she would make it. But it was in vain. No one came. I kept holding my brother's hand in one of my hands, and my mother's hand in the other for hours after they were dead. I could feel how their hands were getting colder and colder." Sami couldn't continue and broke into tears.

My wife, mother, and I were all in tears. We also knew we were in real danger, but we couldn't do anything about it. We couldn't leave the house and go anywhere else. We couldn't get help if any of us were shot. And suddenly the firing started all over again. From the sound, we knew that only Israeli machine guns were shooting. The Palestinian gunmen were all inside the Church of the Nativity. We could hear the tanks moving outside our home, scratching the walls of our compound. The tanks were too huge for the narrow alleys of the Old City, and they were stuck between our wall and that of the neighbors. We could also hear Israeli soldiers shouting in Hebrew. Then the tank at the entrance of our home started shelling. We threw ourselves on the ground, crawling to the other room.

Suddenly we felt the earth shaking under our knees. It wasn't only the tanks outside. Something must have happened to our building inside. The electricity went out. We were in the dark, except for a thin light entering through the bottom of the door. Shells must have penetrated our building.

At this moment, we were more concerned about our lives than the building. Would we survive this invasion? Would we get out of this building alive? We had expected the church compound to give us some protection. We had thought of the Israelis as civilized people who care about historical buildings. But we had been mistaken.

At this point, though we didn't know it until much later, the whole community had begun to worry about us. The telephone rang again. Every time it rang, we were afraid that the Israeli soldiers outside might hear us and start firing at us without warning. The wireless phone was not working for lack of electricity. My wife crawled to the telephone. She lifted the receiver and could hear my aunt on the other end crying, "Najwa, what happened to Mitri?" My wife was silent. She didn't know what was going on. She looked at me sitting on the ground, holding my daughters in my arms. "He is OK. He is fine. But the situation here is terrible. Our neighbors were killed. Our compound shelled. And we're worried about our lives."

"But is Mitri OK?"

"Yes, he is. Why are you asking?"

"On the TV there's a text message reading, 'Israeli troops shell and destroy parts of the Lutheran compound. A monk is reportedly killed at the compound,'" my aunt answered. The Arabic word for monk is *Raheb*. So the text read, "Raheb is reportedly killed at the Lutheran compound." Everyone in the city thought the same: I must be the person who was killed, since no other *Raheb* (in Arabic, *monk*) is in our compound.

The news of my supposed death spread within minutes throughout the whole region. For hours to come, while the shelling was going on, my wife kept answering the phone. Some people were calling because they were curious to hear what had happened and how I had been killed. Others would call to convey to her their condolences. Our telephone line was busy the whole time, and people who called and got a busy signal were even more worried about our family. It took us two hours to send the TV station a message that I was alive.

I asked the station how the error had happened. The explanation was easy and understandable. They had two news messages. The first read, "Israeli tanks shell and destroy parts of the Lutheran compound." Another, separate news message read, "A monk is reportedly killed in a monastery." The editor thought the two messages belonged together, so he edited them to say, "Israeli troops shell and destroy parts of the Lutheran compound. A monk is reportedly killed at the compound."

Around 7:30 PM on that day, the shooting stopped, after almost thirteen uninterrupted hours. It was very dark, as we still had no electricity and no heat. A chilly wind was blowing through the damaged windows and doors of our parsonage. The telephone kept ringing, interrupting the sound of the wind. People were now calling to congratulate my wife for my safety. These phone calls were our only source of warmth, love, and appreciation of the people.

That evening we went to bed early. We were exhausted, but we couldn't fall asleep. Dana and Tala were afraid to sleep in their bedroom alone, so they came and joined us in our bedroom. My wife said a short prayer with our daughters, and we kissed them good night. We wanted them to have some rest. We feared that the attacks were not over yet. Who knew what that night would bring? It was terrifying to be surrounded by

tanks, soldiers, and snipers who were on alert and ready
to shoot at any given moment. "What if they storm our
home while we are sleeping?" my wife asked me. "What
if they kill us in our beds?"

"One should never take life for granted." I remembered how Dietrich Bonhoeffer, a leading German
Protestant theologian who was captured and later killed
by the Nazis, when in prison had written that he was
taking every day from the hand of the Lord with thankfulness as if it were his last. That is exactly how I felt—
that we had been granted a new life on this day, but
also that the coming night might be our last.

Still, even if we survived, what would happen to me
when I went out and saw all the destruction done to our
town and to our compound? I had been so involved in
the Bethlehem 2000 project, first as a member of the
Municipality Bethlehem 2000 Committee and later in
partnership with the Bethlehem 2000 Ministry. Over
$200 million had been invested in our town to upgrade
the infrastructure, beautify it, and provide for sustain-
able development. I feared that much of this investment
had been destroyed.

Then I started thinking about our compound and all
the projects that had been initiated at the church and
center: the guesthouse, the Old Center, the arts and
crafts workshops, the gift shop and gallery, the new
office building, and the conference and cultural center
that was still under construction. Over $7 million had
been invested by governments, churches, and founda-
tions in our compound alone. More than ten years of my
life and my colleagues' lives were invested here. I wondered, "How much of it is now destroyed? How much
will survive this invasion? Can I face this new reality?

Do I have the courage to see how all that we have been building for many years was destroyed by an invading army in thirteen hours?"

I felt as if a heavy stone were lying on my chest. I was afraid of getting a heart attack. What the attack had shattered was our dream for the future; our visions had been destroyed.

At this moment, I thought of words of encouragement spoken by Jesus, recorded in the Gospel of Matthew:

> Do not fear those who kill the body but cannot kill the soul; rather fear him who can destroy both soul and body in hell.
>
> —Matthew 10:28

As I recalled those words, the overwhelming force of the destruction lost its power over me. My thinking shifted direction. I stopped worrying about what had been destroyed and started to think of ways to rebuild. That same night, I started working on a plan to rebuild whatever was destroyed. Destruction was not the end anymore. There was space beyond. I looked at my wife. I wanted to share these thoughts with her, but she was already asleep, and I didn't want to wake her up.

I felt as if I had been given a new dream in the midst of a nightmare, an appreciation that there would be a dawn after the dark night. That night I learned the art of taking every day with thankfulness from the hand of the Lord as if it would be my last day, while at the same time planning as if the brightest future is yet to come. I realized, "The Israeli military might be able to destroy what we have built, they might kill many of our people, but they will never crush our spirit." With this spirit, I was able to close my eyes into a deep sleep.

Days later, I could finally leave our parsonage and assess the damage done to our compound. I saw that our compound had suffered the heaviest destruction of the whole invasion. That week, I put together a report of the damage:

- Tank shells hit the Cave Gift Shop, destroying the whole lower facade of this building, which was funded by the Church of Sweden and had just been opened on December 9, 1999. In the corner of the glass workshop, another shell created a hole measuring a foot and a half wide and deep. Many of the handmade art pieces, the lighting fixtures, the iron doors, and the show windows were totally destroyed.
- The apartment of our international coworkers experienced light damage to the windows, water tanks, main gate and stairs, and facade.
- The office building, the oldest building on our compound, dating back to 1861, was partly damaged. The main gate was bulldozed by one of the Israeli tanks, several stone arches were damaged by the bullets, and most of the windows were destroyed.
- The Abu Gubran Guesthouse was lightly damaged, including its windows, doors, and interior walls. Hundreds of bullets pierced the stone facade, and it is in very bad shape.
- The Communication and Media Center was heavily damaged outside and inside.
- The arts and crafts workshops, renovated in 1999 with help from the Church of Sweden, were heavily damaged on the outside and inside. The roof of the building

had a hole almost a foot wide. All shutter windows and inside windows were totally destroyed. Many of the artists' works were destroyed; some of the equipment was damaged as well.

- The parsonage was hit, too. The staircase facade, the garage, and the wall and entrance were damaged.
- The church survived the invasion. Thank God, the ancient stained-glass windows were spared, except for one damaged only lightly. However, the 111-year-old wall at the church's entrance was badly damaged.
- The Old Center survived the invasion except for two iron doors on the lower level, three windows, window shutters, and two air-conditioning units.
- The main entrance to the compound and gate was totally destroyed and bulldozed by Israeli tanks. The guardroom had been searched and was lightly damaged.
- Damage was done to the newly finished kitchen, funded by the Finnish Ministry for Foreign Affairs. Without any reason, bullets had been fired at the ceramic interior walls.
- The water, electricity, and telephone lines were damaged.
- Many fixtures, much equipment, and numerous art pieces were destroyed or stolen.

Months later, when the curfew was lifted and our staff was able to meet, the damage remained except for the gate and few doors that we had to replace immediately so as to secure the compound and buildings. We still lacked the money to rebuild, but we didn't want to leave everything untouched. Our compound, which had been a beacon of hope for many, became after the invasion a sign of hopelessness and despair. We didn't want to leave our people with this feeling. We wanted to make a statement reflecting the spirit Jesus Christ was talking about. But what could we do?

Our staff came up with an excellent idea. They suggested that we daily open the gift shop doors, which had been heavily damaged, and hang from them a six-foot-long by two-foot-wide black cloth. In white letters on this banner, we would write our statement: "Destruction May Be, Continuity Shall Be." Though black is a sign of mourning, we wanted this banner to proclaim to our community that we will never give up on our town. Rather, we, like Ezra, Nehemiah, Jeremiah, and many of the other Old Testament prophets, are committed to rebuilding what has been destroyed. Even in the midst of death, we live and hold on to the spirit of resurrection. Many friends, neighbors, and visitors told us how uplifting this message was and how much it meant to them. For many this was more than mere words. It was a sign of utmost significance and an uplifting symbol of our collective spirit.

Within a year and with the help of many friends, we were able to rebuild most of what had been destroyed. The compound has again been a beacon of hope during times of despair.

2

Challenging yet Transforming the Enemy

By Thursday, April 4, 2002, the Church of the Nativity had been under siege for two days. Israeli tanks and heavy military vehicles were stationed in downtown Bethlehem, surrounding the compound of Christmas Lutheran Church.

During this time, we (my wife, Najwa; my two daughters, Tala and Dana; my mother; and I) were in the parsonage on the compound. Like the first disciples after the crucifixion of Jesus, we were locked behind closed doors, fearing for our lives. It was too dangerous to look out the windows or go near any of the doors or verandas. Armed Israeli soldiers were going from one house to another, searching for Palestinian gunmen. They clearly had instructions to go in to destroy. And they were very well equipped for that. They carried special explosives to blow up doors and huge hammers to crush locks and sometimes even to penetrate dividing brick walls. Our fear was grounded in the knowledge that, two days earlier, the same Israeli soldiers had broken into the home of our neighbors, killing two of them—an old woman with her thirty-seven-year-old son, a former pupil at our Lutheran School in Bethlehem. We heard the Israeli soldiers breaking the doors of our other neighbors' houses, too, and we wondered when our turn was going to come.

At 1:45 PM on that Thursday, our hour came. We heard the loud voices of Israeli soldiers in the Lutheran compound. They were on the ground floor, under our daughters' bedroom, breaking the door leading to our youth room. We heard the glass of that door falling. We heard the soldiers enter the youth room. Then we heard loud hammering, which shook the whole house. We wondered what they were doing. Later we discovered that they had been breaking the stone cover of the water well located under that room.

I had to choose my next move quickly. Should I stay in our house until they reached our floor, which probably would traumatize my family, or should I go out, talk to the soldiers, and ask them to leave the church compound—an alternative that might risk my life? I had only seconds to decide. I chose the latter risk. I wanted to spare my daughters the scene of Israeli soldiers breaking into their home—their holy of holies, their small nest that gives them warmth and a sense of security and safety. I wanted to spare Tala and Dana the experience of Israeli soldiers pointing guns at them, searching their bedroom, and maybe humiliating their parents while the girls watched.

But before going out, I moved close to the window. While hiding behind a stone column, I shouted at the soldiers in English, "This is a church property! And I am the pastor of this church. I would like to speak to your commander."

"Where are you? We can't see you!"

"I am here on the first floor. I want to come down, but don't shoot."

My family was following the conversation. Najwa said, "Don't go out. You're crazy. They might kill you." I looked at my daughters. I told them not to be afraid. I gave my elder daughter a video camera and asked her to try to film the scene once I was there. Then I went out, wearing my clerical shirt and collar so I would be identified as a pastor.

I opened the door of the church hall on the ground floor and slowly started walking toward the soldiers. There were twelve soldiers, and they were afraid. The whole time I was there, they pointed their guns at my head. I asked them what they were doing here in our church compound. They replied that they wanted to go to an adjacent building. Their explanation was unbelievable, because that building was on the opposite side of the youth room they were destroying. I told them that the building they were trying to enter did not belong to us, and that there was no access to our neighbors through our compound.

I asked them to please leave our church compound, since it is against international law to carry weapons in a church area. The commander was polite. He asked his soldiers to follow him out. But before leaving the compound, he told me that there were two other Israeli military units in our compound. I asked him to communicate to them that this is church property and that I would like to talk to them. He apologized and said he had no authority to do so and that I should look for them myself.

My family was following this scene from behind the window on the first floor. When they saw the soldiers leave, they were relieved, but only momentarily. They started worrying again as they saw my decision to look for the other units in the compound. I couldn't find them outside. Since this was my first and possibly only chance to check what had happened to and on our facilities, I decided to check our office building. When I arrived there, I discovered that the main iron door of the office building had been destroyed. I started to think of all our computers and the files of our staff, and I wondered whether they had been lost or stolen. Eighteen staff members have offices here. I decided to enter our staff building, but first I shouted, "Hello! Is anyone here?" There was certainly no one on the ground floor, but all doors to the staff rooms were damaged and forcibly opened.

While checking on these offices, I could hear some movement on the second floor, where my office in located. So I shouted again, "Hello! Is somebody here? I am the pastor of the church."

"Who's there? Who are you?" a voice shouted on the second floor.

"*Ani Qomer beknisya!*" I shouted in Hebrew, meaning, "I am the pastor of the church." Two soldiers were waiting for me at the top of the stairs. Slowly I started climbing the stairs.

When I reached my office, I saw that the doors to my office and to my assistant's office had been destroyed. The file cabinets were open, and some of the files were thrown on the ground. One window was totally destroyed, while the other two had been shattered by bullets. In my office I faced fifteen soldiers who were pointing their guns at me. I started talking to the soldiers in Hebrew, then in English. At first they thought I was a foreign member of the clergy, so they behaved better. I told them in English, "You could have behaved as real gentlemen. You could have rung our doorbell. You could have asked me to open any door for you. I would have done it. We have, as a church, nothing to hide." But it seems that such behavior is alien to many of the soldiers, a symptom of the moral crisis of Israeli society.

Then the phone in my office rang. I picked it up, and I could hear the voice of our bishop, Bishop Mounib Younan, on the other end: "Your wife called me. She was scared to death and worried about you. She told me there are soldiers in the church compound. So tell me, what is happening?" When I started talking on the phone with our bishop in Arabic to explain the situation, I could feel the attitude of the Israeli soldiers dramatically changing for the worse. They told me to end the conversation. I told the bishop what they were saying. He said he would contact the Israeli authorities and the diplomatic missions to get the soldiers out of the compound. He promised to call me back shortly.

But that was the last time I was able to speak to the bishop. The phone kept ringing, but I was not allowed to answer anymore. The bishop kept trying to call, and so did my wife. The fact that I could not answer the phone drove them crazy. With every minute that passed, their worry rose. In the meantime, a whole team was working in the bishop's office to contact the church leaders and prime ministers in Sweden and Norway, as well as the U.S. Consulate.

This Israeli military unit was not like the first unit I had encountered. They were really nasty. One of them was still angry at me for speaking in Arabic. He commented on that by saying, "Arabic is the ugliest language in the world." I could sense his arrogance and racism.

I replied, "Then Hebrew must be as ugly as Arabic, since both are from Aramaic roots. We are cousins! Don't you know?" This soldier was from Beit Schemesh, northwest of Jerusalem. He worked as a building contractor and had a few Palestinian employees from Hebron working for him. This was all the information I was able to get out of him. Unfortunately, this was his only experience with Palestinians—as cheap, uneducated Palestinian labor, exploited by Israeli contractors and looked down upon.

I sensed hatred against everything that is Palestinian or Arab when another soldier said, "We will let you pay the price, because you have sided with the Arabs." He, like so many people in the world, was ignorant of our existence, assuming that all Arabs are Muslims. He was bewildered when I told him that I am not only a Palestinian Christian, but also an Arab Lutheran pastor.

Another soldier told me, while destroying a painting, "You have here a very beautiful facility."

I said, "We love beauty. We worked so very hard to make this place beautiful. And we take daily care to keep it like this."

Another soldier started making fun of me: "You sound like a very wise person."

I answered, "The real wise person is he who can transform his enemy into a neighbor, and not his neighbor into an enemy."

The commander obviously did not like my answer at all. He shouted at me to shut up, and he ordered his soldiers not to talk to me anymore.

So here I was, sitting in my own church in my own office, but under detention. I was unable to move. I couldn't answer the phone, and now I wasn't even allowed to speak to my jailers. I was alone; there were fifteen of them. I was without any weapon; they were equipped with the latest models of guns and arms. For the whole time, I tried my best to engage them in a dialogue. I wanted to penetrate to their humanity and, at the same time, I wanted to challenge them to see my humanity.

As I sat there thinking of all of this and of the commander's reaction, I asked myself, "Why did the commander get so angry when I was telling him about the wisdom of transforming the enemy into a neighbor?" I wondered if the Israeli military people fear the human in us Palestinians more than anything else. Perhaps our humanity is a mirror that shows them who they have really become. Our humanity shows them their ugly side—the side they try to hide, to avoid, and to flee.

Over two hours had passed since I had entered my office, and I was still under detention. While reflecting on this, I could hear footsteps climbing the staircase to the first floor, where we were. I could see that the Israeli soldiers were becoming anxious and trying to position themselves to attack whoever was climbing the stairs.

As it turned out, the person was an Israeli military commander. He wasn't from the same unit, but I could see from the decoration on his uniform that he was a high-ranking military person. He asked for the unit's commander, who happened to be on the roof. They sent one soldier to call him. And when the unit commander came, this higher commander ordered him to release me immediately. The commander from the rooftop wanted to argue, but the newly arrived officer, a colonel, would

not let him. The commander ordered his soldiers to prepare to leave our building.

I stayed; I wanted to make sure that the soldiers
really left. Then I asked the colonel to go around with
me so that I could check on our facilities. He politely
agreed. We went around the compound, and I was
shocked to see the destruction of our compound: walls
destroyed, doors damaged, windows shattered, computers vandalized. When the colonel saw what had
happened to our facilities, he was visibly embarrassed
by what the Israeli soldiers had done. He even tried to
help me to at least temporarily secure some of the main
doors and windows on the streets so that no one would
come in and steal furniture, computers, and paintings.

This higher commander was polite, but it seems to
me that he had, in contrast to the other unit, received
clear instructions to be polite. As I learned later, our
bishop had succeeded in contacting the prime ministers
of Norway and Sweden, who called the office of the
Israeli prime minister, Ariel Sharon, and asked him to
release me and order his soldiers to leave the Lutheran
compound. Later I discovered that the name of that commander who detained me was Mike Aviad. Before
invading Bethlehem, he had orders to seize the Lutheran
compound and use it as a base for deeper forays into the
Old City. All together it seems that during these two
days, April 2–4, more than 300 Israeli soldiers were
using our facilities as their base. I was glad that the
international intervention led to new orders and pres-
sured the Israeli soldiers to finally leave the compound.

After securing the site as much as I could, I returned
home. My wife, mother, and daughters were anxiously
waiting for me. When they saw me approaching the

door, they all ran to hug me. My mother touched my cheeks to be sure her son was really alive. Najwa put her arm around me, as if she were afraid I might leave again. Tala and Dana hovered around me with joy in their eyes.

This experience was tough for my daughters. They couldn't sleep that night. At 11:00, they still wanted to talk. I had a long discussion with them. I asked them if they thought that what I had done was the right thing. They told me they had been very worried about me, that for some time they even thought of the worst that could have happened to me—that they might not see their father alive again. But they also told me they felt proud when they saw me standing unafraid in front of all those soldiers pointing their guns at me. We discussed how to evaluate a situation and how to calculate risks. I thought that if they grow up in this region, they must learn how to deal with these issues while they are young. Who knows when they will need to quickly evaluate difficult situations and take calculated risks?

When we finished talking, the night was already ending. I kissed Tala and Dana good night, praying for their protection that night and for a new, peaceful day.

One of the Palestinian gunmen leaves the Church of the
Nativity after the settlement is reached

3

Father Amjad and Muhammad under Siege

Finally, on May 10, 2002, after more than five weeks, the standoff at the Church of the Nativity ended. A negotiated settlement was reached after active intervention from the U.S. State Department. Some of the Palestinian gunmen, including some civilians, were sent into exile. Others were sent to Gaza, and the rest of the civilians were released to go home.

While all of this was taking place, a curfew was still imposed on Bethlehem. My family and I, who live only three blocks away from the Church of the Nativity, were like the rest of the world following these events on CNN. On the evening of the day the standoff ended, the curfew was lifted for a few hours, and people started streaming through the streets of Bethlehem to get to the church to see firsthand what had really happened there. Manger

Square was full of European diplomats, international journalists, and hundreds of Palestinian Christians and Muslims.

I left home, too, and walked through the narrow streets of the Old City to see for myself the condition of the Church of the Nativity. On the way, I met many people of different ages, social backgrounds, and political affiliations. As I walked, I would greet acquaintances, stopping here and there to hear what people were thinking about the standoff. Everyone I met was happy that this chapter was finally closed, relieved that the curfew had been partially lifted, and hoping to be able to move on with life. Also, everyone I met was talking about the impact of the standoff on interfaith relations, each from a different perspective. While hearing their views, I was amazed at how the same issue can be interpreted so differently and how the same facts can be related to each other in such diverse and even adversarial ways, creating a new picture every time.

The first people I met were shocked at the behavior of the Israeli soldiers, the cranes, the sound bombs used to frighten those inside the church, and the fact that the Israelis did not even allow food to be brought to the monks and civilians in the church. Others were angry at the Israeli automatic sniper guns put on the cranes and fired at people who were trying to move within the vicinity of the church. I heard one person say that this had been the first time in history that the church of Christ's birth had become a place of death. Six young Palestinians were killed within the church compound during the siege, and it took long and tedious negotiations finally to get the dead bodies out of the church's sanctuary.

One person was angry with the "western Christians," who did not do enough to end the siege and to pressure Israel. He said, "What do you think would have happened if the Jewish Wailing Wall had come under such a siege by Muslims? Do you think the world would have tolerated it this long?"

Another group was angry with the gunmen who sought refuge in the church, the majority of whom were Muslims. One said, "Why didn't they go hide in their mosque? Why use our church for that?" A few people volunteered an answer, saying, "As Christians, we should be proud that Muslims feel more secure in our church than in their mosque."

One man gave a different answer: "If they had hidden in the mosque, Israel might have just destroyed the mosque without thinking twice about it, and the issue would not have had the same impact in the media. The people would have been easily labeled as Muslim terrorists and easily exterminated by Israel. Didn't Israel even try to portray the siege as Muslim gunmen who were holding the Christian priests hostage?"

Another man said, "I agree. And thank God, this Israeli media propaganda simply failed. However, those who sought refuge in the church could have behaved better. Did you see the dirt they left behind them in the sanctuary?"

Someone answered, "Yes, I saw it, and I helped clean it. But can you imagine being in a place with 200-plus people—sleeping there, eating there, having no extra clothes to change, being too afraid of the Israeli snipers to open the doors for fresh air, being afraid to take out the trash, and then being locked in for over forty days? What do you expect the church to look like after that?"

Clearly, it's very difficult to reconcile these points of view because they have to do with each speaker's perspective, religious, political, and social. However, each person I met would tell me, "Thank God that it's over. Hopefully, the curfew will be lifted permanently now so that we can move around." Everyone's concern was daily life. All the people, irrespective of their ideology, wanted to move on with their lives.

Nevertheless, even after the end of the siege, the curfew imposed on Bethlehem continued for another ten weeks. The siege of the Church of the Nativity was over after forty-plus days, but the siege of our town has continued for years.

A few days after the end of the siege of the church, the patriarchs, bishops, and heads of almost all Christian churches in the Holy Land came as a group to Bethlehem to visit the Church of the Nativity. They came to see firsthand what had happened there and to visit our church, Christmas Lutheran Church, which experienced much damage and destruction. I gave them a tour of our compound, and we concluded with a short prayer at our sanctuary. I then walked with them to the street to say good-bye.

After I had finished shaking hands with them, our Muslim neighbor, the shopkeeper across from our church, approached me and said, "Tell me, Pastor, was Father Amjad one of your visitors today?" I replied, "No, he wasn't, but I know him well." Father Amjad is a young Roman Catholic priest at St. Catherine. He is a Franciscan friar who lives in the compound of the Church of the Nativity.

Our neighbor continued, "I would like to ask you a favor. Can you introduce me to him the next time he comes to visit you?" I was curious why our Muslim neighbor was so eager to meet this Roman Catholic priest. He felt my curiosity, so he explained, "I'm not sure if you heard that my son Muhammad was among those who were under siege in the Church of the Nativity."

"No, I didn't know that."

"Well," he continued, "my son belongs to Hamas, the Islamic resistance movement. When the Israelis invaded Bethlehem, he wanted to defend the city. He then fled with everyone else to the church, but he didn't have a weapon. He was one of those deported to Gaza. We didn't hear from him much while he was in the church. However, the moment he arrived in Gaza, he called us to say he's doing well. I asked if he needs anything, but he said he's doing fine.

"During the same conversation, Muhammad said, 'I need only one single favor from you. Promise me you'll do it!' I said, 'I promise. Just tell me what you need. Even if you ask for my eyes, I will give them to you.' Then my son said, 'Promise to look for Father Amjad at the church and to thank him for me.'"

My neighbor explained this unusual request by telling me the story of his son's experience during the siege. While Muhammad was in the church, he became very sick, but the Palestinians in the church had no medicine whatsoever. Father Amjad heard that Muhammad was sick, and he came to visit him. It was the first time this Palestinian man had ever had a private visit from a priest. Father Amjad asked Muhammad how he was feeling—about the symptoms of his illness and about his pain. Muhammad was moved by the priest's concern for his health.

Before saying good-bye, Father Amjad looked into Muhammad's eyes, took his hand, and said, "Don't be afraid. Let me see if I can find some medicine for you at our monastery." In less than an hour, he returned with some medicine and said, "Take this three times a day. I'll pray that you will be well soon." After that, the priest returned often to see how Muhammad was doing.

The shopkeeper told me, "My son said, 'You see, Dad, this is why I want you to go look for Father Amjad and thank him for all he did. He saved my life, and I will remain indebted to him.'"

He also told me he asked his son about the stories of how some of the gunmen in the church had behaved. Muhammad answered him, "What you heard is to some extent true. Not all of the people who fled to the church behaved according to the spirit of the place and in respect for the house of God. I wasn't proud of some of my colleagues. I even had a fight with some of them on this issue. In fact, I lost respect for those few who call themselves Muslims and didn't behave accordingly and didn't appreciate the hospitality provided to them by the church. Some of my colleagues wouldn't talk to me anymore. But I won a new friend: Father Amjad."

As I listened to this story of Muhammad and Father Amjad from our Muslim neighbor while standing in front of his shop opposite our church, I thought, "What a powerful story! But who will hear about it? Probably no one will talk about it. It will definitely not receive any coverage on CNN, nor on any of the news channels. But we all need these positive stories to keep us going." We Christians, Muslims, and Jews need these heroes of the dialogue of life so we can keep dialoguing. We need to lift up all the Muhammads and all the Amjads who quietly strive for dialogue in our midst.

On that day, I promised myself I would tell this story. This book is one way I'm fulfilling that promise.

4

Though War Rise Up against Me

Easter Sunday, March 31, 2002, just a few days before the invasion, our congregation in Bethlehem had met at 10:30 AM to celebrate the feast of the resurrection of Christ. Despite the joyous occasion, people were very worried. Most of the Palestinian towns had been invaded by Israel, and we knew that it was only a matter of days until the Israeli troops would also invade Bethlehem. In spite of this concern, the voices of our church members were joyful as we concluded the service with the famous Easter hymn by Charles Wesley:

> Love's redeeming work is done. Alleluia!
> Fought the fight, the battle won. Alleluia!
> Death in vain forbids him rise. Alleluia!
> Christ has opened paradise. Alleluia!

Then, two days later, as I described earlier, the gates of hell seemed to open. Israeli tanks invaded our city early in the morning, guided by Apache helicopters and orchestrated by the latest communication technology. Palestinian fighters resisted for a short time and retreating later to the Church of the Nativity. Then a siege of the Church of the Nativity began. The Israeli occupation army imposed a twenty-four-hour curfew for six consecutive weeks, from Easter to Ascension. No one was allowed to leave home for school, work, or shopping, except for a few hours each week. Entire families—tens of thousands of people—were forced to stay home, desperate and afraid. During this period, I learned to receive every day with thanks from the hand of the Lord, yet at the same time to plan, dream, and work hard as if a bright future were yet to come.

Only after these weeks of curfew were we able to gather again as a congregation to worship. On this occasion, I chose for my sermon a text from Psalm 27. This is what I said to the congregation:

"Forty days have passed since we last met. Forty days is the period between Resurrection and Ascension, the period when the first disciples stayed behind locked doors and shut windows due to fear (John 20:19). For the same period, we stayed under siege, while the occupying forces destroyed our roads, surrounded our churches, and terrorized our children.

"Forty days were the spring season that was stolen from us. Our cities were invaded at the end of winter while we were still in our winter coats and sweaters. We just came out yesterday from our homes, wearing light summer clothes, as if we have been transported in a wink from winter to summer.

"Indeed, it is the spring of our lives that was stolen from us. We missed seeing the splendid view of the red lilies covering our fields. We missed enjoying the green of the meadows and feeling the excitement of life bursting from our fields, mountains, and valleys. Being held captive in our homes, confined to our television sets and radios, which added to our suffering, we were deprived of enjoying the spring's golden sunshine and denied the usual excursions and school trips.

"We arrived this morning to begin this holy service by reading a psalm we deeply venerate:

> The LORD is my light and my salvation;
>   whom shall I fear?
> The LORD is the stronghold of my life;
>   of whom shall I be afraid?
>   —Psalm 27:1

"A psalm we like, yet as we read it today, we suddenly see it strange to us and far from our experience, as if it does not apply to us or to other human beings.

"Have you not heard the author of this psalm saying:

> When evildoers assail me
>   to devour my flesh—
> my adversaries and foes—
>   they shall stumble and fall.
>   —verse 2

Yet we should admit that the tanks of the occupier conquered the cities of the West Bank within a few hours, much faster than the 1967 Six-Day War. Nothing and no one was able to stop the occupier's tanks, armored vehicles, and war machines.

"History will record that, if we exclude Jenin refugee camp, the occupation forces lost nothing in this war except two soldiers. This might increase the occupation's appetite to repeat the invasion again and again. Indeed, how remote the author of this psalm is from our situation. Have you not heard him saying these words?

> Though an army encamp against me,
>   my heart shall not fear;
> though war rise up against me,
>   yet I will be confident.
>
> —verse 3

We listen to these words, and we become astonished. Someone might say that David had high morale and was very brave.

"In the time of electronic war, a war that our children and we live through, there isn't much room for high morale. The buzzing of the unmanned surveillance planes that invaded our space, that pierced our ears, was proof of this electronic war. Another example of this was the electronic camera monitoring the automatic machine gun that was placed on a crane at Manger Square, a gun that shot dead one of the young men in front of the gate of St. Catherine's Church of the Nativity.

> Though an army encamp against me,
>   my heart shall not fear;
> though war rise up against me,
>   yet I will be confident.
>
> —verse 3

We hear these words and wonder if they belong to someone who takes war and its pain lightly. Don't these words remind us of statements made by some officials in the Palestinian security apparatus or speeches made by some political leaders who said, 'We are ready for any invasion, and we will turn our cities into tombs for them'?

"Don't these words sound as if they are coming from a foolish young man who has no life experience? Don't they sound as if they are the words of a man in a midlife crisis, boasting in front of a group of women to prove his masculinity?

"*No,* you author of this psalm. We fear war as we fear its slogans. War is ugly, offensive, and dangerous, very dangerous. We are not happy to hear some young Israeli and Palestinian men calling for war on satellite television stations, as if it were a piece of Arabic sweets.

"*No,* you author of this psalm. We fear war. War is destructive; it does not differentiate between green and dry, or between good and evil.

"*No,* you author of this psalm. We fear war, not because we want to surrender, but out of wisdom, foresight, and thoughtfulness.

"We say, 'Woe to a nation that sees in war a way to establish domination.' We say it to all the nations in our region, the Israeli, Palestinian, and Arab nations.

"We have proved to one another that our Palestinian youth are able to transform the Israeli coffee shops into tombs and the Israeli youth are able to transform our roads into garbage dumps.

"War is expensive, and the author of this psalm knew that. For we hear him saying, 'My father and mother forsake me' (verse 10).

"Many of you saw Sami Abdeh, the neighbor of this church and a former pupil of our school, wandering the streets of this town, clinging to every native and foreigner he saw and every reporter and journalist around him, telling them, 'My brother and mother left me. They were killed in our house. They remained there for twenty-plus hours bleeding! And no one is taking me up' (Psalm 27:10). Those who saw Sami and heard his cry realize how awful war is!

"Those who saw our children being deprived of their education and enlightenment know how costly war is, for it is closely tied to darkness and ignorance.

"Those of you who saw families in need of bread and a source of income, standing in long lines to get emergency food supplies, understand how humiliating this war is to human dignity, except for that of a few warlords.

"Indeed, you author of this psalm, we fear war very much. War is a blazing fire, and the worst of it is that some fundamentalists, Arabs as well as Americans, feed this fire for their own internal reasons. Yet we are the ones to be burned. Have we all learned? Do we understand that war is not a wedding party where we dance to its rhythm each time some Arabs start clapping for us on television stations? Nor is it a wedding party for the Israelis, who think they have to stand up and select the groom whenever American Jews pay the bill.

"Indeed, you author of this psalm! War does scare us to death, yet ultimately we don't fear it, because it cannot separate us from God, our Lord.

> If my father and mother forsake me,
> the LORD will take me up.
> —verse 10

Even during wartime we say, 'God will take us up.'

"Have we not felt the presence of the resurrected God among us, even in the midst of the shelling and curfew? Have we not felt his merciful hand holding us?

"Yesterday I met with many members of this church, who told me, 'We've missed church. We've missed chanting hymns. We're anxiously waiting to be together, praying together, chanting together.'

"Indeed, war could not separate us from our Savior. Therefore, we sing, 'The LORD is my light and my salvation; whom shall I fear?' (verse 1).

"Indeed, war is not victorious over our Savior, nor consequently over us. On the contrary, war has increased our longing for God. It has strengthened our commitment to our Savior. It has reinforced our conviction for peace and justice!

"War does not scare us; on the contrary, it has brought us closer to one another and assembled us from all over the world: Palestinians, Americans, Germans, Norwegians, Swedes, and Israelis.

"Indeed, you author of this psalm, war does not scare us, because it cannot steal our dream of freedom, the dream of independence and salvation. War cannot steal our vision of a better future.

"We will rebuild the roads that war destroyed. We will replace Bethlehem 2000 with Bethlehem the Future. We will plant new trees in place of the ones that war uprooted.

"War cannot disrupt our plans. It may delay our plans for a few months, but it will not destroy them. War will not rob us of our vision to live in peace with our neighbors. War does not achieve its goals, and because of that, it does not scare us.

"We will continue planting and harvesting, building and constructing, teaching and educating, and drawing rainbows in the sky.

"Indeed, you author of this psalm, war will not scare us. Rather, it has taught us that we must not leave our streets as an open field to 'wedding shooters' and that we must reclaim our streets. We will not leave our future in the hands of the ignorant, but we will roll up our sleeves and assume responsibility for our villages and towns.

"Indeed, war taught us that no nation can be built without honesty. There will be no future without justice, the rule of law, transparent systems, accountability, and democracy.

"War has increased our resolve not to leave the arena to the others. Rather, all of us must become engaged in building a new homeland. We cannot accept that politics becomes foolishness. We will not accept chaos that will bring us misery. Rather, politics is justice, planning, responsibility, law and order, and all of us are called to be engaged.

"For peace is a cumulative process. It is one stone built on top of the other. Renaissance is an accumulative process, and we will not allow anyone to disrupt it. Progress is a cumulative process. A nation cannot move one step forward and two steps backward. War will not scare us, because we have been burned by its fire, learned from it, held on to our dreams, taken on our responsibilities, and deepened our faith. To paraphrase Paul: "O war, where is thy sting? O war, where is thy victory? Thanks be to God, who gives us the victory through our Lord Jesus Christ."

I will always remember this first service after the invasion. We were joined by friends from Sweden, Germany, and the United States and by three Jewish Israeli peace activists.

The three Jewish Israelis from the peace camp were unsure whether they should come to Bethlehem. They wondered whether we would receive them after all that

their military forces had done to us and to our compound. I told them they would be welcome. We can distinguish between the Israeli occupying forces and
Jewish neighbors. During this first service after the
invasion, we sang the same hymn with which we had
concluded our Easter service:

> Love's redeeming work is done. Alleluia!
> Fought the fight, the battle won. Alleluia!
> Death in vain forbids him rise. Alleluia!
> Christ has opened paradise. Alleluia!

After our survival of that Israeli invasion, the words of
this song acquired a new meaning. Christ, the Messiah,
fought our struggle, and no one else. We have no need to
follow any other Messiah, neither Ariel Sharon nor Yasir
Arafat. They fight their personal fights, not ours.

When young Israeli men found the strength to refuse
to serve in the military in the occupied territories, that
was a moment of true Easter feast. And when we, as
Palestinians in the midst of an Israeli invasion, welcomed
our Jewish friends as neighbors, clinging to the vision of
two peoples coexisting in peace with justice and dignity,
then love's redeeming power was really at work.

5

Obeying Commands or Commandments

It was Sunday morning, December 1, 2002, the first Sunday of Advent, the first day of the season of preparation for Christmas. Around that time of the day, downtown Bethlehem is usually crowded with young men in their jeans and women in their beautifully embroidered traditional dresses. The voices of the shopkeepers are very loud as they try to sell fresh fruits and vegetables.

On that morning, and as usual on Sunday mornings, I was sitting in my office overlooking the main street. What I saw was unusual. The city was empty, the streets were deserted. No shops were open. No people were out walking. No voices or other noises could be heard, only odd silence, a kind of silence that was crying toward heaven. I thought of the prophet Jeremiah, who wrote these words:

> How lonely sits the city
> that once was full of people!
> How like a widow she has become,
> she that was great among the nations!
> She that was a princess among the provinces
> has become a vassal.
> She weeps bitterly in the night,
> with tears on her cheeks.
>
> —Lamentations 1:1–2

The silence was disrupted every now and then by the sound of two Israeli armored vehicles roaming the streets. Mixed with that was the voice of an Israeli soldier announcing curfew with a megaphone, saying, *"Mamnou' attajawul,"* which means, "Moving is forbidden. Leaving homes is forbidden." In effect, they were telling us, "You are prisoners. Stay where you are; otherwise you are violating the 'holy' and strict military rules and will be put in prison." When curfew is imposed, schools close, businesses stop functioning, and clinics shut their doors. It is a state of wholesale imprisonment. The curfew that Israel imposes on many Palestinian towns and villages is in effect twenty-four hours a day, seven days a week, and it affects all aspects of life. In the case of Bethlehem, the curfew affects 135,000 citizens, half of whom are children. During 2002 Bethlehem was under curfew for almost four months.

Once the two Israeli military armored vehicles announcing the curfew left the square on which our church is located, I sneaked out to ring the bells of Christmas Lutheran Church at 10:00 AM. Although the distance between my office and the sanctuary is less than thirty yards, it was still very dangerous to defy the curfew under such circumstances. The church member who takes care of our church and the bells lives half a mile away. There was no way he could come that day. I rang the bells, calling people for worship. For me, this was an act of nonviolent resistance. We will not let the Israeli military steal from us the sound of bells calling for worship.

As I rang the bells, I had little faith that anyone would show up. Knowing how Palestinians caught violating the Israeli-imposed curfew are humiliated, my expectations for that Sunday were humble. Every Palestinian is familiar with the stories about Israeli soldiers who ordered people caught violating the curfew to take off their clothes and go back home naked. Some Palestinians were taken prisoner by the soldiers when out during curfew, some had to pay thousands of shekels as penalty, while others were beaten, humiliated, or even tortured.

At 10:30, the Reverend Sandra Olewine and I met at the church's entrance for worship. Although we weren't sure if anyone would be able to make it to church on that Sunday, we still put on our purple Advent stoles. We rang the bells for a second time, marking the start of worship service. Seven people had already gathered in the sanctuary. One of the young people asked if the day really was the first Sunday of Advent, since he didn't see the traditional Advent wreath with its four candles for the four Sundays of Advent. Because Bethlehem had been under curfew for ten days, we had been unable to get pine branches to weave the wreath. We had to miss the music of our organ, too, since our organist lives nearly a mile away from the church and could not make it under such a curfew. Yet, even under curfew and without a wreath or organ music, we still wanted to celebrate the Advent or Coming of the Lord.

At 10:40, I looked at the pews and couldn't believe my eyes. Twenty-seven people had gathered in the sanctuary. I knew how dangerous it was to be on the streets. However, more than two dozen people, young and old, had come to celebrate the first Sunday of Advent. On that Sunday, those members of Christmas Lutheran Church had decided to leave the homes they had been stuck in for many days, homes that were becoming more like tombs guarded by soldiers, to go out and worship the one Lord and live the power of resurrection.

As we gathered, we read the words of St. Paul assigned for the first Sunday of Advent:

The night is far gone, the day is near. Let us then lay aside the works of darkness and put on the armor of light.

—Romans 13:12

How challenging and comforting were these words.

The words are challenging, since the "night" of the thirty-five-year occupation has been very long and feels endless. The day of freedom and dignity seems very far away. How else can we explain the arrogance of the Israeli occupation, which reoccupied Bethlehem shortly before the seasons of Advent and Christmas, demonstrating that the Israeli military do not care for the Christian world? If they wish, they can smash the "little town of Bethlehem." It is too little, compared with the might of their tanks.

Yet there is comforting good news in St. Paul's words—the night has lost its power. The gospel calls us and empowers us to cast off the works of darkness and occupation. The light of right is stronger than the power of might.

The presence of the church members, in spite of the curfew, was the best expression of that light. When confronted with the choice between obeying the commands of a military occupation or the commandments of their Lord, the church members chose to "obey God rather than any human authority" (Acts 5:29). They made their choice, knowing that they might pay a heavy price.

Life under
Occupation

6

The Land That Swallows Its Children

No other conflict in the world receives as much media attention as the Israeli-Palestinian conflict. Almost no week passes without some breaking news from this region. Yet the life span of breaking news is short. A story might last for a few minutes, a few hours, or a few days, and then comes the next story. People move on quickly to the next issue, next topic, next region, and next item on the news agenda.

The Israeli-Palestinian conflict is also the longest ongoing conflict in modern history. News has been breaking from this region for more than a century. Generation after generation is born, grows up, lives, and dies while the conflict continues. While breaking news focuses on a particular moment, zooming in to cover a certain highlight or crisis of the conflict, the news coverage seldom looks at the conflict from a wide-angle perspective.

A wide-angle perspective shows what the conflict does to people's lives from womb to tomb, and how it is affecting generation after generation. An end to the conflict is, unfortunately, not in sight.

Everything and the only thing I have known in my life, and still do, is living under the Israeli occupation. Looking back, I can clearly see how this occupation has affected all major stages of my life so far. It is interesting what people remember from their own childhood. In fact, I don't remember much. However, my first and oldest memory goes back to the year 1967. I was not yet five years old when the Six-Day War broke out. About the Jordanian rule before that, I have no memory whatsoever. But I can still remember June 5, 1967.

The first sounds I remember are those of Israeli airplanes flying over our town, followed by the sound of an explosion, which shook our house. An Israeli bomb was dropped on the home of our nextdoor neighbors, penetrating the roof over their living room. The landing of this bomb a few feet away from our home was a message for my mother that our home was no longer safe. The safest place, my mother thought, would be the Church of the Nativity.

My father had another opinion: "If I have to die, I want to die at home." He refused to go to the church. I remember him sitting in one corner of the house, close to the radio, following the news as events unfolded. My mother grabbed my hand, collected some food, and took me to the Church of the Nativity. I remember entering that big, dark, windowless room packed with dozens of people, mainly women and children. Some were lying on mattresses, others were cooking on a gasoline stove, and still others were discussing politics.

We stayed in the church for a few days, and when we came out, Israeli soldiers were on our street, searching one house after another. For me, this was the day when the Israeli occupation started.

I don't remember much about living under the Israeli occupation during my early childhood, except for the October 1973 war. In contrast, my years in high school were shaped by demonstrations, tear gas, and school strikes. At the time, as a teenager I was not interested in politics. I don't recall participating in any of the demonstrations organized by students. Nor was I engaged in clashes with the Israeli army. We did organize a strike at school, but that was about it for me. My focus was on my studies, my reading, my hobbies, and my youth work at church.

In 1975, when I was only thirteen, my father died. My goal was to continue my studies while running my father's bookstore.

My mother was eager to attend my high school graduation. Yet she was to be disappointed. Although I finished my high school classes with very good marks, I never graduated. During my last year of high school, one of our classmates, Samir, a church member and a good friend, was caught by the Israeli soldiers during a demonstration and put in an Israeli jail. Toward the end of that school year, all of our classmates gathered to discuss when and how we would have our graduation ceremony. After a long, heated discussion, we decided to cancel the graduation ceremony altogether. Many couldn't imagine graduating while Samir was in prison. How would his parents feel on that day? We wanted to show solidarity with Samir and his family. For some, this decision also involved economic considerations. The cost of the graduate's clothes, reception, and party was more than some families could afford. Still, the decision was difficult. Parents who were looking forward to seeing their kids graduate were disappointed. I know that this was how my mother felt. She never forgot that, because of the conflict, her only son never graduated officially from high school.

My goal was nevertheless to continue my studies. I wanted to study theology so I could come back and serve my people. I was lucky to receive a scholarship from the Lutheran World Federation to study in Germany. I started my higher education at the Mission Seminary in Hermannsburg. In the summer of 1987, I submitted my doctoral dissertation at the Phillips University in Marburg and returned to Bethlehem.

A few months later, on December 9, the first Intifada started. The daily clashes between Israeli soldiers shooting and Palestinian kids throwing stones were taking place just outside our church and house. Many Sundays I had to interrupt my sermons because the shooting outside the sanctuary was louder than my voice. Church elders as well as students from our church were imprisoned without charges or trial. Political realities would again affect an important stage of my life's journey. During the Intifada, I met my wife, Najwa. Najwa was a member at Christmas Lutheran Church. Her sister Nuha and I were in the same confirmation class. I remembered Najwa from our church youth retreats back in the mid 1970s. But in the late 1980s, she was working at Bethlehem University as an accountant. We met at an organizing meeting for an international youth gathering. One year younger than

me, Najwa is very pretty, self-confident, and hard-
working. We fell in love and after a year, we decided in
early 1989 to get married. Still the Intifada continued.
The Israelis had killed hundreds of Palestinians.
Thousands of Palestinians, including church members
both old and young, were in Israeli jails. The united
political leadership of the Intifada issued statements
asking people to refrain from holding any dancing parties or other joyful celebrations and receptions.

Najwa and I discussed this issue. What should we
do? Should we postpone our wedding? If we did, how
long would we have to wait until the Intifada ended? No
one could predict how long it would last. Should we just
go ahead and marry without a wedding party? Knowing
that we marry only once, we wanted our wedding to be
a very special time. We wanted to celebrate the occasion with friends. At the same time, because I am a pastor and religious leader, we didn't want to be insensitive
to the feelings of the many friends and acquaintances
who had lost loved ones or whose sons, daughters, and
husbands were in jail. After long discussions, we
decided not to wait, but rather to go ahead and marry
without the celebration. We promised each other we
would make up for the party later. Maybe we wouldn't
wait until our twenty-fifth anniversary. We thought we
would have a party after half that time—twelve and a
half years of marriage.

We were married in a school chapel with over a thousand guests. The sermon delivered at our wedding service focused more on the Intifada than on our marriage.
We thought that the topic chosen was inappropriate for
the occasion, since it sounded as if a commitment to a
life together was similar to going to war. So we married

without a party, just as I had finished high school without a graduation celebration.

After twelve and a half years, when the time came for our agreed-upon celebration, the political situation was even worse. We were under curfew. Today, after fifteen years, we're still waiting for the right time to celebrate our wedding publicly.

In 1989, when Najwa and I married, I was still hoping to see the end of this conflict during my lifetime. There was a sense of optimism in the air in spite of everything. Yet when my first daughter, Dana, was born a year later, Saddam Hussein had just finished occupying Kuwait.

I remember the night in January 1991 when the allies attacked Iraq and Saddam fired his first missiles on Israel. A friend called to share this breaking news. I felt that my heart would break. Dana was only four months old. She was sleeping in her tiny bed. I picked her up and rushed with her to the so-called sealed room. My wife followed me. She closed the door tightly behind us. Then she took Dana in her arms while I was sealing the room with tape from the inside. I clung to the radio to hear the news.

My main concern was whether the Iraqi missiles being fired in our direction contained any biological weapons. The Israeli military did not distribute gas masks to Palestinians, as if to say we didn't deserve to live. I was ready to die. But I kept looking at my little daughter while asking myself, "Why should she die so young? Why should she be here?" I thought of my father, who had been ready to die in his home in 1967 but let me go to the church for protection.

When my second daughter, Tala, was born, the Oslo Accord was almost one year old. It was said that when

Prime Minister Yitzhak Rabin and President Yasir Arafat shook hands on the lawn of the White House on September 13, 1993, they were actually thinking of their children and grandchildren. My hope, too, was that if we did not have the life we had desired, at least our children will have life, and have it abundantly.

When Tala entered school on September 3, 2000, the future somehow still looked bright. The Bethlehem 2000 celebrations were at their peak. Yet a few weeks later, after the provocative visit of Ariel Sharon, then the Israeli opposition leader, to the Haram as-Sharif in Jerusalem, the second Intifada broke out. Accompanied by hundreds of soldiers, Sharon visited the third most holiest place in Islam. Palestinian Muslims felt that this was a desecration of their holy site. Demonstrations erupted everywhere and continued to spread throughout the West Bank and Gaza, leading to deadly clashes with the Israeli army.

Whereas the symbols of the first Intifada were mainly Palestinian youngsters throwing stones and Israeli troops firing at them with tear gas, rubber bullets, and live ammunition, the symbols of the second Intifada were Palestinian gunmen, Israeli tanks, Apache helicopters, and F-16 fighter jets. In October 2000, Bethlehem got a taste of what this means. At the time of the first attack of the F-16 on our neighborhood, I was watching TV, following the news. I heard the sound of the F-16 coming closer and closer with incredible speed, then striking a compound just three blocks away from our home. We felt the air pressure strike our windows and doors. The same moment, the electricity was cut off. It was late evening and already very dark.

My younger daughter, Tala, was in her room during this time. When the lights went out, she started screaming in terror. I called her by name, telling her not to be afraid, that I was on my way to her. I felt my way in the darkness. My eyes slowly adjusted to the darkness, and moonlight was shining in Tala's room. When she saw me, Tala ran to me and threw herself into my arms. "Don't be afraid," I said. "I am with you. I won't leave you." I kissed her cheek and pulled her closer to my heart. I sat in the darkness, holding her for a while in my arms.

While I was talking to Tala, trying to conquer her fears, my own heart was full of fear. I kept asking myself, "Will the day come when Dana and Tala will hold their sons and daughters in their arms during a new round of Middle East turmoil? How many generations have to go through these experiences of war and shelling that my father's generation, my generation, and now my daughters' generation have gone through?" I wonder if the day will ever come when the land will stop swallowing its children. I pray that they will be able to graduate, celebrate their weddings, and share with their children memories of the good old days.

7

A Matter of Life and Death

The phone rang at 5:30 on Sunday morning, January 4, 2004. The sound frightened us, because when people phone that early, it's almost always an emergency. Congregation members who call early in the morning usually want me to pray with them or take Holy Communion to a relative who is dying. I wondered who it might be this time; I wasn't aware of anyone who was in serious condition.

My wife answered the phone. After a moment, she cried out, "Has something happened to Father?" My father-in-law, who had suffered fainting spells every few months, had been to the hospital several times. This time it wasn't a fainting spell but a very painful stomachache. My sister-in-law had called to ask what they should do. They had called an ambulance, and it was already on its way to their home.

The first problem was where the ambulance should take my wife's father. There aren't many hospitals in Bethlehem. There is one maternity hospital operated by Caritas, another small private hospital that is poorly staffed, and King Hussein Hospital. This third hospital started as a Lutheran hospital opened in the nineteenth century by the Jerusalem Verein, an organization related to the Swedish Church. It was later taken over by the British government and then by the Jordanian government, which renamed it King Hussein Hospital. King Hussein's governmental hospital is the only general, public hospital in the whole Bethlehem region, serving a total population of almost 130,000 people. Although many donor countries, especially Italy, have invested a lot in this hospital, it has a poor reputation among the general public. People complain about the hospital's poor medical service, a shortage of well-trained doctors on its staff, an underdeveloped infrastructure due to a lack of resources provided by the Palestinian Authority, and weak commitment of employees and patients to the hospital's mission. No one would choose this hospital if there were an alternative.

A few outpatient clinics operate in Bethlehem, but they operate during the daytime only, and none of them is equipped for real emergencies. This is typical for Palestine, where one finds many small clinics providing bits and pieces of services. Almost no medical facility exists for providing serious and comprehensive treatment.

In the 1980s and 1990s, people could go to one of three Palestinian hospitals in Jerusalem (the Augusta Victoria Hospital, operated by the Lutheran World Federation; St. Joseph's Hospital, run by the Catholic

Sisters of St. Joseph; and al-Maqasid Hospital, a Jerusalemite hospital funded by an Islamic trust).

In sum, we had few choices of where to take my father-in-law. I recommended going first to the emergency room at King Hussein Hospital to find out whether he had anything serious, and from there deciding what to do next. A Red Crescent ambulance took my father-in-law to that hospital. I showered quickly, dressed, and drove hurriedly to meet them there. My father-in-law had just arrived, and the nurses were checking his pulse and asking him about his symptoms, medications, and so on. They did a cardiogram and took a blood sample.

After almost an hour, the young doctor on duty couldn't find anything wrong with my father-in-law's heart, so he ordered that my father-in-law be sent to the men's ward. My brother-in-law and I had to push my father-in-law on the gurney to take him to the third floor. We entered the ward, and I couldn't believe what I saw. In one of the rooms, a middle-aged patient with a long beard was preaching in the Islamic tradition to many other patients who gathered around him. Patients are vulnerable, and it's easy to use their pain and suffering to ask them to repent. I supposed that this man was a member of an Islamic party. These parties are not only political; rather, they cater to people in their hour of need, grief, and anger to sell them some sort of salvation. They are where the people are. This is how they recruit followers.

We passed this group performing Morning Prayer and looked for a nurse to tell us where we should take my father-in-law. A young nurse showed us a room, saying that it had the only empty bed in this section. We entered the room, and I had my second shock. The bed-sheet was used and dirty. We should have brought a clean sheet from home.

When we asked about the specialist who was to come and check my father-in-law's condition, we were told that no one was there so early, but someone would come later in the day. Seeing all of this and observing my father-in-law's intense pain, I decided we should move him from this hospital to St. Joseph's Hospital in Jerusalem as soon as an ambulance was available. By then it was almost 6:30. My brother-in-law called the Red Crescent to ask if an ambulance was available to drive his father to Jerusalem. The answer was that ambulances are not allowed to enter Jerusalem that early but that around 8:00 AM an ambulance might be allowed to enter.

I headed home from the hospital after that, leaving my brother-in-law with his father. It appeared that my father-in-law wasn't suffering from anything serious, and in a matter of two hours, he should be in good hands in Jerusalem. I went home to prepare for the Sunday service, while my wife left home to be with her father.

At 8:00 AM, my wife, brother-in-law, sisters-in-law, and mother-in-law expected the ambulance to arrive for them. But it didn't show up on time. When they called the Red Crescent, they were told that the driver wasn't in yet. Finally, at 9:00 AM, the ambulance showed up at the hospital.

"Does the patient have a permit from the Israeli military authorities to enter Jerusalem?" the driver asked.

My brother-in-law answered, "Yes, he has a valid permit from 5:00 AM until 7:00 PM. But his wife doesn't.

Do you think the Israeli soldiers at the checkpoint will let them through?"

"No one knows. It depends very much on the mood of the soldiers," the driver told him. My father-in-law was put into the ambulance, and my mother-in-law joined him. My wife and her brother and sisters kissed him good-bye, and the ambulance drove away toward the main checkpoint at the northern entrance of the city.

My wife came back home, angry that the ambulance had been late and worried about her father's condition, especially the intense pain he was experiencing. Yet she was a bit relieved to know he was on his way to a better hospital and soon would be getting better attention and diagnosis.

The route from King Hussein Hospital to the checkpoint is less than half a mile, not much farther than from the hospital to our home. Within less than five minutes, the ambulance had reached the checkpoint. No other cars were there, so the driver was optimistic they would get through quickly.

However, the ambulance had to wait until the soldiers' mood dictated the driver should bring the vehicle closer for inspection. Fifteen minutes elapsed, and still they waited for a sign from the soldier. Finally, the soldier signaled them to come closer. He looked at the driver and asked him where he was going. "To the hospital in Jerusalem. I have a patient who is in great pain and needs to get there," the driver replied.

"Does the patient have a permit?" the soldier asked.

"Yes, he has! Here it is."

The soldier took the permit, a sheet of red paper, about six by eight inches. At the top was the title, "Entry Permit to Israel." Under that was my father-in-law's name, Sameer Elias Shehadeh Khoury, together with his identification number. The permit was valid for three months, and the reason was stated as well: business. Sameer, my father-in-law, was a businessman. He owned a travel agency and a restaurant before he emigrated to Michigan in the late 1970s to become an American citizen. Later he came back to Bethlehem, where he reopened his restaurant and with a few others started a hotel not far from the checkpoint. Because he was a hotel owner who needed to go to Jerusalem to look for business and groups, and as someone who was seventy-four years old, he occasionally obtained permits from the Israelis to enter Jerusalem. (In fact, my father-in-law's hotel, Bethlehem Inn, has been occupied by Israeli soldiers since October 2000. They placed Israeli snipers there, prohibited any of the owners from entering it, and transformed it into a military headquarters. The Israeli military justified the hotel's occupation as "for military purposes." No doubt, the occupation of his property affected my father-in-law's health. And the soldier who stopped the ambulance at the checkpoint might have stayed that night in my father-in-law's hotel.)

He looked at the permit in his hand and said to the driver, "This permit isn't valid."

The driver said to my father-in-law, "I thought you told me that you have a valid permit to Jerusalem."

My father-in-law answered, "It is valid. Read the date carefully. It's still good for the next few weeks. Can't you read?"

"I can read," the soldier replied. "No problem with the date. But here it says that the purpose of the entry is business. Today you aren't a businessman, but a patient. For this reason, the permit isn't valid. You are not allowed to enter."

By that time, my mother-in-law was becoming more and more worried about her husband and more and more impatient. "But we are American citizens. Here are our American passports. As such, we cannot be prevented from entering Jerusalem."

"Your American citizenship does not count if you are Palestinians," the soldiers replied. "Go back, get a permit, and then come back! Turn around quickly."

"You do not fear God? Don't you see that this old man is in pain?"

It was clear by that time that the soldier was in a bad mood and there was no chance of entering. Therefore, the driver decided to try his luck at the other checkpoint to the west of Bethlehem, less than a mile away. So the ambulance turned around, drove back, passing again by King Hussein Hospital, and climbed up the hill, driving through the town of Beit Jala to reach the so-called DCO checkpoint.

The ambulance had to stop again and wait for the soldiers before approaching. The soldier there was somehow quicker than the soldier at the other checkpoint. Again, the soldier asked for my father-in-law's permit, read it, and gave it back. "The patient can enter Jerusalem, but not this ambulance," the soldier said.

"But this isn't the first time that we've entered Jerusalem with this ambulance," the driver said.

"No, the ambulance is not allowed."

Arguing with the soldier did not prove helpful at all, so the ambulance driver suggested calling another ambulance from Jerusalem to come to the checkpoint and take my parents-in-law to the hospital. The driver called a Palestinian ambulance from Jerusalem.

In half an hour, the Jerusalem ambulance arrived at the checkpoint. It backed up to the checkpoint and stopped back to back with the Bethlehem ambulance. The drivers carried my father-in-law from one ambulance into the other, and the ambulance quickly left the checkpoint to Jerusalem.

By then it was close to 11:00 AM. In less than thirty minutes, the ambulance arrived at St. Joseph Hospital. Once my mother-in-law stepped into this hospital, she felt relieved. Finally, they were in a better situation. What a difference from the other hospital—clean bedsheets, smiling nurses, caring doctors. She was confident her husband would get the treatment he deserved. She thanked God they had finally reached their goal.

Two doctors were already waiting for him. They performed a cardiogram and several other tests. "His situation is very serious. Why didn't you bring him here earlier?" one doctor asked my mother-in-law.

"The soldiers at the checkpoint didn't let us through," she explained. Then she asked, "But how serious is his situation? What is he suffering from?"

"He had a severe heart attack a few hours ago. His heart muscles are damaged to a large extent. His chances to survive are very low," the doctors answered.

"There is no hope at all?" my mother-in-law asked.

"There is always hope in God, but his situation is very serious, and you should know that. If he survives, then it would be only through a miracle!"

Twelve days later, on January 16, 2004, my father-in-law died in the hospital. He was seventy-four years old. His only son had not been allowed to enter Jerusalem to visit him. His daughters and I had been granted four-day permits, twice, to visit him during daylight. Sameer, my father-in-law, died of a heart attack because of nonexistent professional health services in Bethlehem and because of the Israeli checkpoints.

He isn't the only one who has died for these reasons. Almost daily this same story repeats itself. The poor health services in Bethlehem and the checkpoints around our city are matters of life and death. When we buried my father-in-law, I wondered what would happen if I were to have a heart attack one day. Where could I go, and how would I survive the checkpoint? In Bethlehem, almost everyone has the same worry.

8

Adventures in Driving

I still remember getting my driver's license back in 1989. At that time, it took me quite a while to get through the complicated bureaucracy of the Israeli military, which was still in charge of the whole transportation ministry. The first Intifada, which started on December 9, 1987, was still going on. Israel was exercising collective punishment measures, which included postponing driver's license tests, complicating licensing procedures, and delaying paperwork.

In front of every transportation bureau, applicants formed long lines, standing outside under the sun in summer for hours and under the rain in winter for days, only to be sent away at the end of the day with such excuses as "The computer isn't working" or "The person in charge isn't on duty" or "The boss isn't in to sign the document." I spent hours and days just to get my license and then later to register my car. But finally I had my driver's license and a car. I was ready for my first and, as it turned out, my last long drive.

My aunt and her son were visiting us from Michigan, and I wanted to show them the country. My aunt had emigrated in 1968 to the United States with her family, and her son had not been back since. He left as a teenager and came back as a businessman. After all these years, he was eager to see what his homeland looked like.

Having a driver's license and a car, I invited my aunt and her son on a trip to the Galilee. We left Bethlehem, drove five miles to Jerusalem in the north, took a right turn, and drove fifteen miles east, down through the Judean desert to Jericho. Jericho, situated almost a thousand feet below sea level, is the lowest city in the world and is very hot in summer. But it is one of the most beautiful winter resorts. As we drove through Jericho, my wife showed my aunt the restaurant where she used to come with her family every Sunday for lunch. We had a long journey before us, so we didn't stop there but continued north through the Jordan Valley. We drove about 100 miles on a single-lane road. To the east, on our right side and beyond the Jordan River, we could see the Hashemite Kingdom of Jordan. At the end of that road, we approached Tiberias, a city with black volcanic stone houses built by Herod the Great on the western shore of the Sea of Galilee in gratitude to Tiberius Caesar.

In a restaurant in Tiberias, we enjoyed the famous St. Peter's fish. Opposite us, on the eastern shore of the sea, we could see parts of the Golan Heights, a Syrian territory occupied by Israel in 1967. While we sat there, my aunt told of how, before the 1948 war, her family used to drive from Jerusalem to Beirut, the Lebanese capital, to have a good fish lunch on the Mediterranean. From there, they would drive to Damascus, the Syrian capital, for coffee and the famous Syrian sweets, and continue afterward to the Jordanian capital, Amman, where they would dine. Then they would drive back the same day to Jerusalem. This was, my aunt told me, less than a day's drive.

It sounded to me like paradise—a life without borders, where people could travel for hours without permits, and where people and goods could move freely from one place in the Middle East to the other.

"We have to move on," I told my aunt. "We still have to visit Nazareth and then drive from there back to Bethlehem." We would have loved to stay in Tiberias for one or two extra days, do some sightseeing, and drive up to the Lebanese border, but that was forbidden to Palestinians from the West Bank and Gaza. In 1989, we could still visit Israel, and my aunt and her son, as American citizens, could have stayed there overnight. However, my wife and I were not allowed to do so. For that we needed an extra permit. I didn't want to bother applying for such a permit, knowing that the application would take hours, if not days, of standing in line at the Israeli military offices, perhaps being interrogated and often humiliated as if we Palestinians were not humans with flesh and blood. It was easier to take a one-day trip and maybe return the next day to the Galilee than to apply for a one-night permit.

So at the end of the day, we drove back from Nazareth through Jenin, Nablus, and Ramallah to

Bethlehem, another 120 miles. Everyone enjoyed this one-day 300-mile trip from Bethlehem to the Galilee. But not in my wildest dreams would I have ever foreseen that this was to be the longest trip I would ever be able to make with my car in the Holy Land. As the years pass, this trip will seem like a story from a golden era.

Two years later, such a trip was no longer possible for Palestinians. In 1991 and after the first Gulf War, Israel erected the so-called checkpoints around our cities, preventing us from entering Israel without a permit. In 1991 through 1993, it was not too difficult to get such a permit. The permit would allow a person to drive to Jerusalem and often to Israel as well, with the exception of Eilat, an Israeli resort city at the northern edge of the Red Sea. The permit would be given for a minimum of a few hours to a maximum of three months. It specified the license plate number of the car, the ID number of the driver, and the hours within which the person could travel (usually from 5:00 AM to 10:00 PM). Passengers in the car needed to have their own personal permits.

After the Oslo Peace Accords were signed on the lawn of the White House in Washington, D.C., on September 13, 1993, we expected that peace would free us from the requirement to obtain permits to enter Israel and that we would be able to visit the neighboring Arab countries, as in the good old times my aunt had told me about. Yet what happened was the opposite. After Oslo, it became very difficult and later even impossible to get a permit to travel with one's own car into Israel or even to Jerusalem. It became more and more difficult to get a personal permit, even without the car, to travel to Israel. Most of the permits issued during this period allowed Palestinians only to travel the five miles to Jerusalem, using only public transportation and during limited hours from 5:00 AM to 7:00 PM.

As a result, every time I needed to go to our church headquarters in Jerusalem, I had to call a taxi and pay $20 for the trip back and forth. I was prevented from going to Israel, even for holding our church summer retreats in Nazareth as we used to do. However, we were still allowed to travel within the West Bank to go to Jericho, Hebron, and Nablus. Traveling to Jordan was easier during this period as well.

With the start of the second Intifada on September 28, 2000, the situation continued to deteriorate. During the first months of the Intifada, the Israeli military started closing all the roads surrounding our cities and villages, so that all roads leading out of or into Bethlehem, for example, were blocked. It was very difficult to travel to Ramallah, to Hebron, or later to any other city or village. Big, heavy rocks were put at the entrance of each town and city. The only way to move around was to leave one's car on one side of a roadblock, climb over the roadblock, and then take another car on the other side. To go from Bethlehem to Hebron, a fifteen-mile drive, a person needed to change cars and taxis three to four times, depending on the situation.

Therefore, during the last three years, I've been able to use my own car only within a two-square-mile area. Most of the time, it has been almost impossible to get a permit to travel to Jerusalem, not to mention Israel. And it became even more difficult for us to travel to Jordan.

We basically have been prisoners in our own towns and villages. At the same time, Israel started building twenty-four-foot-high walls, with trenches, buffer zones, barbed wires and sensors around many of those cities and towns, including Bethlehem, transforming them into ghettos, like the homeland areas of South Africa's apartheid era.

But even our cities and villages, which were made into prisons and ghettos for us, were in the eyes of the Israelis still a luxury. In 2002 Israel started imposing curfews in our towns and villages. For days and weeks, we were forbidden not only from driving through our towns and villages but also from walking in our own streets.

Imposing a twenty-four-hour curfew seven days a week on the Palestinians became very natural for Israel to do. For weeks and even months, our homes became our prisons. During 2002 to 2003, Israel imposed on 150,000 inhabitants of the Bethlehem District, including my family and me, curfew for almost seventeen weeks. Our children were not allowed to go to school; our workers were not able to come to work. Our immediate concern during that time was to ensure that when the curfew was lifted, we would rush to the nearby supermarket to buy food and then return before the Israeli soldiers reimposed the curfew.

The world community often expresses concern about our humanitarian situation and asks Israel to loosen the restrictions imposed on us. I wonder what we can expect. Merely ending the curfews would leave many other travel restrictions. Dare we hope only to be able to drive within a two-mile radius as before or to go to Jerusalem with a permit? Should we be grateful to drive to other cities in the West Bank without permits?

We don't expect more. The United States hasn't asked for more from Israel. And Israel, even with those minimum demands, has to reflect on and assess the situation before agreeing to comply. If we Palestinians behave, we might experience a "generous" gesture. If we don't behave, Israel will impose another curfew on us. As Palestinians, we are supposed to learn that our lives depend not so much on God but on Israel's grace, generosity, and gestures of goodwill.

9

What Would You Do If You Were in My Shoes?

A few years ago, I planned a trip to the United States, together with my wife, who holds a U.S. green card. We had been invited by friends and fellow Christians from Florida, Illinois, Kansas, and Missouri, who were anticipating our visit as much as we were. They worked very hard for three months to arrange for me to deliver a series of lectures, preach, and attend important meetings. However, at the end of the day I was to leave, I found myself sitting in my office in Bethlehem, writing of my experience instead.

To understand our situation, consider what it would take for an average American to travel abroad. What would you need besides a valid passport, a visa, and an airplane ticket? Not much more. Yet, for a Palestinian, travel is totally different. A Palestinian can't leave the country without a travel permit. For me, living in Bethlehem, these permits are issued by the Israeli military based in the illegally built settlement named Gosh Ezion, located six miles south of Bethlehem. Yet how can one reach Gosh Ezion if Bethlehem is sealed off and one is allowed to drive, in a car with a Palestinian green license plate, in a one-mile radius only? First, I had to get a taxi with a yellow license plate to travel on one of the so-called bypass roads built on confiscated Palestinian land yet designed mainly for use by Israeli settlers. I met the taxi on December 28 at one of the many roadblocks the Israelis have set up to divide the Bethlehem districts into pieces. Once we reached our destination, my wife and I submitted our applications, and we were told that Palestinians wouldn't be allowed to leave the country unless they had another foreign passport besides their Palestinian one. Nevertheless, we were instructed to come back in three days to see whether we could get our permits.

On December 31, I called the Israeli military authority to ask whether we had been granted the permits. I was told that my wife had received one but I had been denied. The reason given was that my wife has an American green card and I do not. I told them that I, as a clergyman, have a Vatican passport. The soldier said, "Then you should fill out new forms, attach a copy of your passport, and apply again." I went to a special office that had these forms and filled out a new application, as the soldier requested of me.

My wife and I drove again to the roadblock to catch a yellow-license-plate taxi but discovered a small opening in the road that would allow our car through. I decided to take the chance, and I drove my own car toward the settlement. During this six-mile journey, we were afraid of what might happen to us if a settler decided that our presence on the road was not to his or her liking. Finally, we reached our destination and got our permits. We returned to the roadblock and tried to get back in the way we had gone out, but an Israeli military vehicle was standing there. A soldier beside the vehicle pointed a gun at us and told us to go back to the place we had come from. I told my wife not to worry and that we should go to the other roadblocks to see if there were any openings.

It was then that we started our Via Dolorosa, traveling from one roadblock to another. For more than an hour, we continued, and I kept thinking about how villagers commuting to Bethlehem every day suffer as a result of the town being sealed off. Finally, we found an opening in one of the roadblocks and were able to enter our town before the soldiers saw us and closed it.

On January 4, we headed at 9:30 in the morning in a yellow-license-plate car to the Ben Gurion Airport, which is around thirty miles northwest of Bethlehem, to catch our 4:35 PM flight. The soldiers at the entrance of Bethlehem stopped the car, asked for the permits, checked them, and allowed us to go through. We arrived at the airport early and were the first in line. We handed our passports, tickets, and permits to the security official, who looked at the permits, then at us, and at the permits again. She told us that our permits were not valid and that we could not fly. "But the people who issued them reassured me yesterday on the phone that they are," I argued. She said she would check with the airport police, who told her that the permits were invalid.

Being prepared for anything, I had the phone number of the military authorities who issued the permits, and I called them. I spoke to the captain, who reassured me that the permits were valid. I handed my cell phone to the security officer so she could hear it for herself. She sent another officer to the airport police, and that officer returned with the answer: *No Palestinian is allowed to leave the country.*

"Let me talk to the police authorities myself," I said.

The security officer replied, "You should look for them yourself. Try the information desk." In the meantime, her boss arrived and shouted at her for wasting her time talking to us.

She left, and I started my search for the police, leaving my wife at the counter with the luggage. I was prohibited from getting to the airport police, because only travelers with a boarding pass can reach them. Finally, I was told to walk to the police headquarters, located outside the airport's main building. Once I got there, they wouldn't let me in. The woman at the desk dialed a number and handed me the phone. I explained to the policewoman on the other end what had happened, and her answer was *"No Palestinian is allowed to leave the country.* These are our instructions." She refused to take the number of the military authorities to talk to them and insisted that they should call her.

I called the military authorities again and asked them to talk to the airport police. The person I spoke to promised to do so. And for the next three hours, our Via Dolorosa continued between the military authorities, airport police, and airport security. At 3:35 I called the captain at Gosh Ezion, who told me that he had tried his best, but that there were orders, which he could not overrule, so we could not travel that day. He said I should wait until things calm down. I wondered, "How can things calm down if they continue treating people that way?"

What would you do if you were in my shoes?

I'm not referring to the financial loss, the taxis, and flight tickets. Nor am I writing about lost time and stress. Rather, I desire basic human rights of free movement and of living in dignity.

Many Palestinians, especially Christians, choose the option of emigration. They leave to live in the Promised Land of the United States, thus emptying the Promised Land of Palestine of its resources, potential, and promise. Others are radicalized by such treatment. The constant inhumane treatment eliminates their imagination of a better life here and now.

What would I, Mitri Raheb, do if I were in an American's shoes? I would press my government to make sure that the Palestinians have real sovereignty and control over their borders, their bypassless roads, and their airspace, so that tomorrow not one single Palestinian would be treated the way I was treated. I'm not talking about luxury but about dignity: living without humiliation. I would follow the footprints of Christ and do everything possible to bring justice, healing, and hope to the land in which two thousand years ago the Divine gave humanity its new meaning, dignity, and promise.

The Bearer of Burdens by Suleiman Mansour

10

Carry On

On the wall in my office hangs a poster reproducing a famous painting by Suleiman Mansour, a Palestinian Lutheran artist who is a graduate of our school in Bethlehem and currently lives and works in Jerusalem. The painting, entitled *The Bearer of Burdens,* is one Mansour did in the 1970s. It shows an old man, a Jerusalemite, one of those who used to be waiting at the Old City gates to be hired to carry heavy items into Jerusalem. Since no vehicles can enter the Old City because of its narrow streets, people living there depended very much on these strong men to carry their furniture or other belongings through the Jerusalem bazaar. The way such a man carried a heavy item was usually by wrapping a thick rope around it and carrying the item on his shoulders, while circling the rope around his head and holding its ends with both hands. The heavier the item was, the more the man stooped. In the painting, this old man is carrying something unusual: the whole of Jerusalem, with its Dome of the Rock, churches, and dwellings. Carried on the old man's shoulder, Jerusalem has the shape of an eye, symbolizing the importance of Jerusalem for the Palestinian people.

This painting is one of my favorites. Often while sitting in my office, overloaded with work, I gaze at this old man carrying Jerusalem. You can sense that he is determined to carry on with his mission; you can sense his patience and perseverance. But you can also sense that the need to carry heavy items all of his life has made him seem older than he really is. The tiredness of all those years has left its marks on his face, and the daily hardships he has faced have made his hands very rough.

Often I sit and meditate on the painting. How much can a person carry, and for how long? Every person has to carry a cross in life, but when does a cross become so heavy that the one carrying it will just collapse under it, as Jesus did while walking the Via Dolorosa? At one point Jesus could not "carry on" anymore. He collapsed under that heavy burden and needed someone to come and help him carry the cross.

How long can we as Palestinians carry this heavy burden of occupation and still carry on with our lives? For how long can we handle such a burden of harassment, humiliation, invasions, closures, and confiscations without collapsing and getting crushed underneath it? It is not that we Palestinians are unwilling to carry our cross. But we are humans who can carry only so much.

As Palestinians, we are suffering to some extent because of disastrous policies of some of our leadership during the twentieth century. We are paying a heavy price for their miscalculations, for following false prophets, and for ill management. Before we blame anyone else, we have to blame ourselves. We have to confess our sins and face the consequences of our wrong deeds. We have to confess that many of our political leaders were either not sincere or not up to the tremendous challenges facing us. We have to confess that many of the tactics used by some of our people were devastating for us: the militarization of the Intifada, the use of guns in our otherwise nonviolent struggle, and the suicide bombings against civilians.

But our burden is much heavier than the total sum of all of our sins. As Palestinian people, we continue to carry on our shoulders not only our sins, but like the servant of the Lord described by the prophet Isaiah, we carry on our shoulders the sins of many other nations as well:

> He was despised and rejected by others;
>> a man of suffering and acquainted with infirmity;
> and as one from whom others hide their faces
>> he was despised, and we held him of no account.
> Surely he has borne our infirmities
>> and carried our diseases;
> yet we accounted him stricken,
>> struck down by God, and afflicted.
> But he was wounded for our transgressions,
>> crushed for our iniquities;
> upon him was the punishment that made us whole,
>> and by his bruises we are healed.
> All we like sheep have gone astray;
>> we have turned to our own way,

and the LORD has laid on him
    the iniquity of us all.
He was oppressed, and he was afflicted,
    yet he did not open his mouth;
like a lamb that is led to the slaughter,
    and like a sheep that before its shearers is silent,
    so he did not open his mouth.

                        —Isaiah 53:3–7

As the suffering servant, we often feel "despised" and "rejected". We are labeled by some with all possible and impossible stereotypes. Yet more and more people in the world are beginning to understand our suffering and our "acquaintance with grief." Many people in many countries are starting to sympathize with our human and just cause. Others decide "to hide their faces" from us and not to take a position at all in this conflict. But very few understand what is really happening to us.

We suffer because of our own sins, but also because of the sins of many others. We suffer because we have to pay the price of the sins of Europe against the Jews. Europe was not capable of integrating the Jewish community within its own borders. European governments persecuted the Jews in a series of large and small horrors leading to Auschwitz. Many in Europe still carry heavy guilt feelings for what their ancestors did to the Jews. But to some extent, some Europeans deep down feel relieved that the Jewish people finally have their own state outside of Europe. Indeed, we have to pay the price of Europe's sin in tensions and conflict in the Middle East. The Holocaust harmed not only the Jewish people but also the Palestinians, who became the victims of the victims.

We also carry the sins of the Jewish people. Those who were traumatized by their experience of persecution developed a hunger for acquisition of more and more power. Israel became obsessed with power. The Israelis hated their former persecutors but deep down were also impressed with them, wanting to become as powerful. The sense of insecurity experienced by European Jews was transformed into a security syndrome. Security became the golden calf of the Jewish state. As Palestinian people, we are paying the price of this Israeli obsession.

Furthermore, we pay for the sins of the Arab world, whose politicians made the Palestinian question the hook on which to hang all their internal problems. Many Arab nations also feel guilt, but toward the Palestinian people. Every day, while dining in their homes, they see live pictures of Palestinians "like lambs that are led to the slaughter" (Isaiah 53:7). They know that their governments pay only lip service to the Palestinians. They know that they are part of the problem rather than of the solution. Through their misguided policies, Palestine was lost and never recovered again. Almost all of the Arab governments have used the Palestinian question to their own political ends. As Palestinians, we still pay the price of these policies.

We also pay for the sins of part of the Jewish diaspora, especially in the United States. Many American Jews have their own guilt feelings. They feel guilty that they continue to live in the diaspora and not in the "Jewish homeland." So they compensate for these guilt feelings by sending donations to Israel and by lobbying for extreme Israeli policies. Backing Israel even in its wrongdoing, subsidizing Israel's continuous occupation of the West Bank and Gaza, and pressuring the U.S.

Congress to support a one-sided pro-Israeli position harms not only the Palestinians but in the long run the Israeli people themselves. And as Palestinians, we have to carry on our shoulders the sins of the Jewish American lobby as well.

Then we have the Christian Right in the United States. I do not find much in them that is Christian or right. They are anxious for Armageddon, no more and no less. They do not even care for Israel itself, but for the final "big bang." Deep down they are anti-Semitic, hating Israel and the Jewish people. But in the meantime, they don't mind sharing a bed with the Jewish lobby, as long as it fulfills their intimate desire for power. They not only support Israel blindly, but they try to back its far-right parties, which call for expansion of the Israeli settlements in the occupied territories and even ethnic cleansing of the Palestinians. Many of them do not even talk or communicate with us Palestinian Christians. They think that we aren't "kosher" enough for them. As Palestinians, we have to carry on our shoulders the burdens of the so-called Christian Right. The further right they move, the heavier our burdens get.

As I continue to meditate on the painting, I feel the heaviness of our burden as Palestinians. But how long can we carry on? How many more burdens can we bear without getting crushed? We do not pay for our own sins only, but for those of many in the world. Salvation will come only if Israel, the Arab world, and the Jewish diaspora, as well as people in Europe and the United States, understand that the Palestinians are paying for the sins of all these groups.

The prophet Isaiah's words about ancient Israel in exile are true also for modern Palestine:

Surely he has borne our infirmities
  and carried our diseases;
yet we accounted him stricken,
  struck down by God, and afflicted.
But he was wounded for our transgressions,
  crushed for our iniquities;
upon him was the punishment that made us whole,
  and by his bruises we are healed.

—Isaiah 53:4–5

It is interesting that the suffering servant is entrusted with wholeness and healing. World peace depends very much on understanding the many burdens that the Palestinian people are carrying on behalf of the world. Healing between nations depends very much on having the world confess its sins and assume responsibility for the present situation instead of simply indulging its guilt feelings.

As Palestinians, we will continue to carry on, carrying all of these burdens until Israel and the world muster the courage to take their share. True liberation from guilt feelings, as well as Israel's own redemption, will come only if and once they see the Palestinian people relieved and free.

Glimpses of Hope

11

The Light of Right, Not the Power of Might

The weeks of October and November 2000 were among the most frightening weeks of the second Intifada. The Intifada then was less than a few weeks old. No twenty-four-hour curfews had yet been imposed on Bethlehem, as in 2002–2003, but life in Bethlehem was terrifying. Every late afternoon, the streets would be deserted. Once the sun set, all public, social, and economic life came to a standstill. For people living on the outskirts of Bethlehem, the evening hours were a time of fervent prayer, watchfulness, alertness, and fear for their lives.

It was becoming routine that in the night, a few armed young Palestinian men would appear in the outskirts of town and fire a few bullet rounds at a Jewish settlement that wasn't even in the range of their fire. What they were doing made no sense to the majority of the population, since the shooting had no political reason or justification. Most of Bethlehem's residents were against these acts, and many viewed the young men as potential criminals or gang members who thought of themselves as some kind of Palestinian Rambos. Not only was it impossible for the bullets to reach the other side, but the Israeli soldiers used the shooting as justification to fire back with heavy artillery on the civilian neighborhoods. The armed men would immediately flee, leaving the innocent civilian population in harm's way.

Instead of following the star leading to the Christ Child, people watching the news would follow the bullets and shells destroying homes of the "little town," as a journalist once described Bethlehem. The town of Bethlehem was once again alight "like a Christmas tree." But for the Palestinian civilians living on the outskirts of town, this was more like the gates of hell opening on Good Friday. These nights became nightmares in the memory of the children, women, and men of Bethlehem. The sun seemed to refuse to shine again and to purposely delay its rise.

Our house is located in the city center, not on the outskirts of our city. Still, we were able to follow what was happening. We could first hear the shooting and tell where it was coming from. Next, we could see the phosphoric bombs lighting that neighborhood, and a few seconds later, we could hear the Israeli tank artillery firing. Our thoughts would immediately go to our friends living in that area, knowing they were in danger.

We knew most of the Palestinian families whose homes were damaged or destroyed by the Israeli shelling. One house was that of our contractor, Jamal; a second was that of Hanna, an anthropologist and a part-time professor at our center for the training of future Palestinian tourist guides; a third was the home of Sami, a dentist and my sister's friend. Many families whose houses were not directly hit fled their homes. Suha, my wife's best friend, could no longer stand living at the outskirts, so she moved to our guesthouse until she could rent a house in the city center, far from the shelling areas. She was not alone in seeking refuge at our guesthouse. Several church members came with their families and stayed, feeling more sheltered in the shadow of a church.

On October 30, 2000, the night before Reformation Sunday, the house of six-year-old Alice, my daughter's best friend and classmate at our Dar al-Kalima School, was bombed. Together with her family, Alice was subjected to a terrifying experience that has scarred her little soul. As the Israeli tanks were shelling their house, Alice and her family tried to flee through the olive groves, only to be further terrified by Israeli helicopter lights, which followed them in their frantic attempt to escape. The same day, Alice and her family became homeless. The three-story building, which took years of hard work to build, was gone in one night. The next day, as we were singing the Reformation hymn, "A mighty fortress is our God, a sword and shield victorious," I thought of Alice and wondered if she, like Martin Luther, could boldly hold on to her faith in this time of tribulation.

Indeed, these were times of great tribulation and fear. When the citizens of Bethlehem awoke in the morning, they would go see whose house had been shelled the night before, checking that all family members were well. After paying a short visit with those neighbors, they would continue on their way to work. In the mid-afternoon, people would leave work in time to quickly do some shopping and arrive back in their homes before sunset.

In the midst of all of this, Advent was approaching. Our staff met and agreed that we had to do something to conquer the fear and take back our streets. We did not want to be just spectators, but rather actors. Even if we could not stop the shooting and shelling, we could raise our voices and send a strong message to our leaders, to our Israeli neighbors, and to the whole world. But how? What would be a strong signal at such a time? What would be the most powerful sign in such a context? After discussing several ideas, we decided to organize a peaceful evening candlelight march.

I knew how difficult such an endeavor would be. The unified political leadership was trying to organize peaceful demonstrations after the Muslim Friday prayers and Christian Sunday services, but with little success. If they who represented almost all political parties had failed to bring fifty to a hundred people together each time, who were we to succeed? And if we were to organize such a candlelight march in the evening, who would dare to walk at night, through the deserted streets, for a peaceful demonstration? Moreover, it would be very risky. What if a few gunmen started shooting while we were marching? What if Israeli gunmen opened fire on the crowd? Who would be able to take such a risk and carry such a responsibility? We wished there were safer options.

In spite of these concerns, there was a convincing argument in favor of organizing such a march. The situation had become so critical that only a bold move could make a difference in people's lives. We felt we had to challenge people to conquer their fear and reclaim their streets and neighborhoods. Nevertheless, we had to be careful and plan the march responsibly. Therefore, we decided to avoid the outskirts of Bethlehem and organize the march in the Old Town, in the city center.

We were already in the Advent season as well as the holy Muslim month of Ramadan, so we decided to use the image of light, which marks both seasons, as the main and only image. We wanted this march to be inclusive. We planned the march to start in Madbaseh Square at Christmas Lutheran Church, continue to the Greek Catholic church, move from there to the Syrian Orthodox church, stop by the Islamic mosque, and conclude at Manger Square in front of the Church of the Nativity. When we arrived at a church, the choir of that church would sing, the bells would ring, and the march would move on to the next stop. At the mosque, the evening prayer was on and we were supposed to wait for the congregation to finish their prayer and join us. We wanted to have only one banner with one short yet precise message: "The Light of Right, Not the Power of Might." People were to carry only candles and to march silently. There would be a sense that we were silently mourning, not demonstrating, celebrating, or chanting.

We conceived of the march as a family march. We did not want only young men to participate. Rather, we wanted whole families with children, women, and the elderly to stress that it was a peaceful and nonviolent march.

All of these ideas were great, but the biggest question was how we would gather people. How many would dare to respond to our invitation? Would they dare to conquer the fear and reclaim their streets in the evening? Clearly, we needed strong partners to carry out this endeavor. We had to coordinate with the political leadership but not to depend on them to mobilize people. The invitation would go out in the name of all the main churches of Bethlehem. The actual organizing, however, was done at the International Center of Bethlehem and in the Catholic Seminary at Beit Jala. Yet, even with all of these preparations going on, we weren't sure how many people would be courageous enough to accept our invitation. Some thought that if only a hundred people showed up, the whole effort would be worthwhile. My thinking was that 500 would be a realistic number. We ordered 1,000 candles and torches in case our faith proved to have been too small.

The date was set for Sunday, December 9, at 6:00 PM, which also would be the second Sunday of Advent. A high-ranking delegation of the heads of mainline American churches, organized by Churches for Middle East Peace, was supposed to be in Bethlehem on that day.

Little time was left for organizing the march. We distributed the tasks among our staff. Some were to contact the churches, others were to mobilize schools and scout groups, a third group would contact and invite the media people, and so on. It was a huge undertaking, and it sounded impossible. Our biggest task was to convince people to conquer fear. It wasn't an easy task at all. I still remember a morning devotion on Thursday, December 6, where I started by asking the children at the school a question: What do you think is easier, throwing a stone at a tank or lighting a candle at night? For the children, the answer was obvious. They felt sure that throwing a stone requires more courage, while lighting a candle is boring and easy. After hearing their answer, I challenged them, saying, "If this is the case, then I expect to see you all, with your parents, at the march on Sunday at 6:00 PM."

The children's response to this invitation was, "No way would our parents allow us or themselves to leave home after sunset."

"You see," I replied, "lighting a candle at night isn't an easy thing after all. It often requires more courage than throwing a stone, and it is certainly more meaningful."

On December 9, 2000, the churches announced the march during their Sunday services and invited their members to participate. In the afternoon, something very unusual for Palestine was happening. People started to gather as early as 5:00 PM. At 5:30, we reached our goal of 500 people. All got their candles and were ready to march. However, we had to wait. The march was to start at 6:00. Several bishops arriving from Jerusalem with the American delegation weren't there yet. At 5:45, over 2,000 people were waiting to march. Only half of them held candles, since never in our dreams had we expected such a turnout. The crowd started moving, and there was no way we could stop them. Our choir sang, the bells of Christmas Lutheran Church rang, and people began to march. It may have been the first event in the history of Palestine to start fifteen minutes earlier than planned.

In this first family march since the beginning of the Intifada, over 2,500 Palestinian men, women, and children and international visitors participated, testifying to the fact that people want to take control over their own lives. The march, which was the largest Christian-Muslim gathering in Bethlehem since the visit of the pope in March 2000, ended with the reading of the following news release in several languages:

> We are marching tonight, Palestinian Christians and Muslims, children and adults, men and women, locals as well as internationals, to break the silence by the world towards an injustice that is committed against our civilians held hostage to Israeli might and aggression.
>
> We are marching tonight to take back our streets, which have been haunted with fear and death in the past few months.
>
> We are marching tonight to tell the world of our continuing fifty-year struggle to realize our self-determination and freedom.
>
> We are marching tonight for the families who have lost their homes to missiles and are now refugees, sleeping in a different place each night. They have joined the millions of Palestinian refugees waiting to return home.
>
> We are marching tonight for our children, who are traumatized by the Israeli helicopters invading our skies and armed Jewish settlers, roaming our streets.
>
> We are marching tonight to protest the military closure imposed on us, causing poverty, misery, and hunger.
>
> We are marching tonight to give a message of hope and light to people around the world seeking justice and freedom.
>
> We are marching tonight to overcome fear and to light a candle for hope.

We are marching in Bethlehem, the birth-place of Christ, to call upon all of you to break your silence and play an active role for the cause of peace and justice, so that the light of the resurrection would shine again upon Jerusalem.

As the text was read on the stage, there stood Alice's mother, Sami the dentist, Hanna the anthropologist, my wife's friend Suha, and many others whose houses had been damaged or destroyed. They all were victims of that power of might, yet they came to witness to the light of right.

Unfortunately, no major international or regional media were present. There were only a young woman from the Austrian television network, who was making a film about our ministry, and two local TV stations. Some of the international journalists might have been afraid to come at night to Bethlehem. They were used to filming Bethlehem "lit like a Christmas tree" from the outskirts of Jerusalem. For other journalists, I was told, a candlelight march is boring. Unless blood was shed, unless stones started flying, unless buses were bombed, such an event would never make it into the mainline news. Good news, it seems, is no news. Media outlets, it seems, care less for the light of right and more about the power of might.

Painting from the Christ in the Palestinian
Context exhibition by Tamer Monir.

12

Christ in Palestine

In November 2002, the Church of Sweden approached me, asking if we had one or two paintings of Christ from a Palestinian perspective. They were preparing an international exhibition for a Swedish audience entitled The Christ of the World, showing different paintings of Christ by African, Asian, Latin American, and other international artists. The exhibition was to have its grand opening in June 2003 at the Cathedral of Uppsala before touring cities, galleries, and churches in Sweden. The exhibition aimed to present the beautiful and colorful world of the Christian church to the Swedes and to say that the church is neither ethnic nor nationalistic, but rather crosses borders. At the same time, the exhibition was meant to offer Swedish parishes a tool for working on their own image of Christ.

Knowing that one of the missions of our center is to work on a contextual Palestinian Christian art, a pastor from the Church of Sweden approached me, hoping we could help him find and identify two such paintings: "As I know your work with Palestinian artists, I'm sure that you are the right person to find the right material. Is it possible for you in this difficult situation to ask artists you are thinking of for this project to create paintings of Christ?"

When I received this request, I was very excited, for it fit perfectly into our mission. But at the same time, Bethlehem had been under twenty-four-hour curfew for weeks, and no one knew when the curfew would be permanently lifted. A twenty-four-hour curfew means house imprisonment. No one is allowed to leave home.

Undeterred, I immediately called our art coordinator, Faten, in her home to see what she thought about the request. We decided that the next time the curfew was lifted for a few hours, we would meet to discuss the idea in detail. A few days later, the curfew was lifted for a few hours so people could do their shopping, and Faten and I met.

After some discussion, Faten suggested that instead of us simply choosing one or two paintings, we should organize a competition for all interested Palestinian artists and then choose the best of their submissions. Faten's suggestion was intriguing, but a question remained: How could we organize such a competition under curfew? Then we thought that curfew might be just the right time to do it. The many Palestinian artists under curfew and house imprisonment have time. Why not challenge them to use all their creativity and imagination? By participating in this project, they could overcome their depression and imprisonment, and we would receive many diverse and good paintings of Christ in the Palestinian context. In a way, organizing the competition under such circumstances was an act of creative resistance.

Faten started preparing to announce the competition. We placed ads in the most widely circulated Palestinian newspaper, but we knew that under curfew, you couldn't really rely on people getting the newspapers. Only the cities that weren't under curfew would get the newspapers; the others would not. From her home, Faten also started contacting the major art centers in the West Bank and Gaza, some by e-mail and others by phone. E-mail and telephone are the best and often the only possible communication tools under curfew. December 18, 2002, was the deadline for artists to show interest and submit a proposal. The deadline for handing in the paintings was set for the beginning of February 2003. For almost the entire time from November 2002 to February 2003, Bethlehem and other Palestinian towns and villages were still under round-the-clock curfew.

On February 6, all paintings were to be exhibited at our gallery. The gallery and the gift shop had been badly damaged during the April invasion of 2002. Yet with the help of a few organizations and churches, we were able to rebuild them even under the most difficult of circumstances. The exhibition, Christ in the Palestinian Context, was to be the first at the reopened gallery. When the opening of the exhibition was advertised, the announcement said, "4 PM on February 6 if curfew is lifted on that day."

By chance or by divine intervention, the curfew was lifted on that day for a few hours, and the opening of the exhibition took place as scheduled. In her opening speech, Faten said, "For almost one year, it was closed and neglected. However, today, al-Kafh Gallery opens its doors once again. In spite of all the destruction, its walls are covered with colorful paintings. Regardless of the curfew regime, it is hosting sixteen Palestinian artists from different places all over the West Bank— Nablus, Ramallah, Jerusalem, Bethlehem, and Hebron. Some of them are well known, while others are still young, beginner artists. What gathered them together was Christ in the Palestinian Context, the topic of the exhibition. Actually, all these artists have participated in a painting competition on the same subject, over-coming by that the difficult situation and the tight closure in which they live. Each artist searched deeply in the personality and life of Jesus Christ and expressed a part of it in relation to his or her own surrounding."

When the exhibition opened, I was in the United States. Only through our Web site, www.annadwa.org, was I able to have a look at the paintings. After reviewing all of them, I couldn't believe my eyes. Of all artists participating, 60 percent who submitted paintings were Muslims. For me, this fact was not so astonishing, since over half of those who attend our programs are usually Muslims. Rather, I was amazed for a different reason. It was interesting to see that so many Muslim artists dared to paint a biblical figure, something that is actually forbidden in traditional Islamic theology and spirituality.

Even more amazing was that all of the Muslim artists except one submitted a painting of the crucified Christ. Only one of the Christian artists had selected the cross as the theme of a painting. A Greek Orthodox iconographer, for example, painted barbed wire preventing Jesus from entering Jerusalem, a reality we have been living for ten years. Jesus shares our story.

Like us, he does not have a "smart donkey" that can fly over the wire. Christ is very human.

I couldn't stop thinking of the fact that the overwhelming majority of the Muslim painters chose Christ on the cross to represent the context they are living in. We know that in the teachings of Islam, Christ was not crucified. For Christ to be crucified means really nothing else than for God to be on the losing end, a situation that is unthinkable in Islam. God is too great to be a loser. Why did these Muslim artists nevertheless paint Christ the crucified? They risked betraying their religion. They took many risks, since all the paintings were publicly exhibited in our gallery for one month.

I could think of but one explanation. When these artists thought of their suffering and what was the most meaningful message for them in that circumstance, they could not but think of Christ the crucified. The message of the cross was for them so powerful that they were ready to risk painting the crucifixion. At that moment, they discovered that the message of the cross is more powerful than any wisdom or religious teaching they had been taught. In a God sharing their bitter destiny, they find strength, comfort, and power. The message captured their minds and imaginations.

A jury was formed to choose the best six paintings. The Church of Sweden decided to buy all six winners, instead of only one. Since June 2003, the six paintings—four by Palestinian Muslim artists and two by Palestinian Christian artists—have been touring Sweden, portraying the story of the Palestinian people.

It is the suffering and crucified Christ who can best speak to our occupied nation in our suffering. And it is he who can best tell our story to the world.

13

Bright Stars

One of my favorite stories in the Bible is a story about Abraham told in Genesis 15. Abraham was wandering as a nomad in the Negev Desert. He traveled with his caravan by day and stayed in his tent by night. His tent was made out of dark goat hair. And although he was well-to-do, his tent was not that big. Abraham was traveling with his wife, but at that time, he had no son yet.

Nights were very frightening for Abraham. He wasn't so much afraid of the wild animals of the desert as he was of being lonely. At night, he would lie down and try his best to sleep, but would stay awake. His big worry was that he would die without having a son to carry his name and inherit his wealth. Without a son, there was no future for a Middle-Eastern man of that time. Without a son, there was no light at the end of the tunnel. Most probably a foreigner, Eliezer from Damascus, would inherit all Abraham owned. All he owned meant nothing to him without a son from his own flesh and blood. Abraham was angry with God, who had brought him out of a fruitful area, Haran, into this desert. Abraham had followed God, hoping for descendants, and here he lay alone. In the neighboring tent was his wife Sarah. The tiny black tent in which Abraham lay symbolizes how he must have felt. Everything was so narrow, everywhere darkness, hopelessness, and loneliness.

Although God tried to comfort Abraham, assuring him that God did not forsake him, it was difficult for Abraham to believe. The reality he was facing—his aging—was speaking a much more convincing language than the words he was hearing from God. At one point, God must have felt that it was hopeless to convince Abraham with words. So God had to think of a tool much more powerful. God stopped arguing with Abraham and instead took him out of the tiny black tent and put him under the wide heavenly tent.

There stood Abraham, surrounded by a seemingly endless desert, with no light whatsoever around him. But once he lifted his eyes up to the skies, he became speechless. Up there he saw an endless tent, decorated with millions of bright stars. The stars looked very near, as if he could reach them and touch them with his own hands. What a difference between being in that small dark tent and being here under the wide heavenly tent, with countless stars shining. *Wow!* was probably the only word Abraham was able to say. But this scenery was convincing:

> And he believed the LORD; and the LORD reckoned it to him as righteousness.
>
> —Genesis 15:6

After the beginning of the second Intifada on September 28, 2000, the situation of the Palestinians in general and Palestinian children in particular looked to me very much like that of Abraham. The horizon looked very dark; there was no light for the future whatsoever. Depression was becoming a major threat to our entire nation. Twenty-four-hour curfews imposed on our towns and villages went on for months. Those curfews made our children, who constitute more than half of the population, feel like Abraham in his tiny black tent. The siege imposed on our towns, which prevented the children from traveling, made them feel like prisoners at home. No trips were possible, since travel from one Palestinian city to another became too difficult. Above all, Israel started during the Intifada to construct a wall around our cities, transforming them into ghettos, leaving the Bethlehem population without any prospect for future growth.

The existing school system does not help kids to look up either. Pupils are just expected to memorize. They need not learn to think, critique, improvise, or create new things. They are left behind without many options.

Our children are left either to watch television, with many violent scenes, or to play war on the streets. Their "stars" have often become gunmen, whose pictures are hanging everywhere in the streets. As a result, the children of Bethlehem have become children at risk.

Inspired by the story of Abraham in Genesis 15, the staff at our center developed a new program, which we call Bright Stars. This program was designed to present an alternative for our kids. We didn't want to use mere words to convince them that they have a future. Rather, we want them to have an experience similar to Abraham's of standing under that wide heavenly tent with its countless stars. Our challenge was how to help our kids resist believing that house arrest is their fate and that a concrete wall is their determined horizon. We wanted them to discover that the skies are their limit.

To do this, the Bright Stars program invited children to gather in different art, music, sports, communication, and environmental clubs, according to their talents and gifts. All of these clubs focus on expressing emotions, fears, thoughts, and visions. The program's creative, holistic approach and the large variety of techniques give plenty of stimulation to stretch the imagination. Children's initial ideas, no matter how insignificant they may seem, are recognized as original, creative thoughts and are treated with the respect they deserve. The children are encouraged to develop their ideas. This fosters the desire to create and participate and helps in the building of self-confidence and self-identity. The children will discover themselves to be the "Bright Stars," talented in music, in sports, and in the arts, as well as in forming a new community.

Children participating in the program are between the ages of six and sixteen. They are Christians and Muslims, girls and boys. They come from different social and economic backgrounds. Some of them are from Bethlehem and the two adjacent towns, a number of them are from neighboring villages, and others come from the city's refugee camps. A feeling of belonging to an inclusive Bright Stars community is being developed.

We started this project in February 2002 with fewer than forty kids. Since then, the Bright Stars community has been growing day by day. In less than two years, we have involved close to 1,000 kids. Our goal is to reach out to 2,000 kids by May 2005. We are on our way, slowly but surely.

Anyone who believes that Palestinians have no future has to come and see this new generation of Palestinian Bright Stars. Here you can see Lina learning karate so she can defend herself nonviolently, Ahmed learning how to make a radio program for kids by kids, and Ramez enjoying training in the swimming pool. Here you can see children carrying their musical instruments—one her guitar and another his oud. Here you can see Nida sitting in the garden, painting flowers, while Amal is fusing glass pieces together. Here you can see Adel learning photography and taking pictures, while his friend Tony is working on a new Web site for the summer academy. Here you can see Fadi playing chess, practicing how to think strategically, while Salaam is taking ballet lessons.

If you see this, you feel that a miracle is taking place. Children raised and growing in a context of war, who are at risk of becoming potential gangsters, are learning war no more. Instead, they are being guided by bright stars, becoming themselves Bright Stars. These are indeed Abraham's descendants. Let's hope their faithfulness will be rewarded with what they deserve: justice.

14

Perplexed but Not in Despair

After the beginning of the second Intifada on September 28, 2000, we received only a few visitors. Before that, especially around the turn of the millennium, we used to welcome a group or two a day on average. The number has since fallen to no more than one group a month. And in contrast to the groups that visited before the Intifada, which were mainly tourist and pilgrim groups, those who dared to come during the Intifada were mainly solidarity delegations of friends, who came to say, "We are with you." Upon leaving, as a way of summing up their visit to Bethlehem, many of the delegates would say something like this:

> We never anticipated the situation to be as bad as it is. The closure, the curfews, the wall surrounding your city, and the economic

situation are much worse than we expected. When you hear about the conditions in the news, they don't seem real. However, once we got here, we saw what a devastating impact they have on the spirits, souls, and bodies of your people. You have to see it to understand it. But we assure you that 'what we have heard, what we have seen with our eyes, what we have looked at and touched with our hands' (1 John 1:1) we will be sharing with our friends and other people back home.

But having said that, please allow us to add another thought. We came here aiming to give you hope and to strengthen you in your struggle, but we leave this place having received more than we brought with us. It is you who give us hope, and it is you, through your many ministries, who strengthen us.

When I ask our visitors what gave them so much hope, they mention mainly two things: the staff of the center and the breadth and depth of the ministries.

The staff of our center is indeed impressive. Not only because most of them are very well educated, and not only because the overwhelming majority of them are young (in their thirties), and not only because most of them are women, but mainly because they stay in Palestine by choice. Many of them could easily emigrate to the United States, Canada, or Australia, as so many of our people have done, but the people on our staff have decided otherwise. In fact, every day they have to make a new commitment to stay in spite of the closures, the curfews, and the humiliation. They are here because they want to make a difference in the lives of their people. They have a commitment to their community.

So many examples come to mind. There's Rana, who, after finishing her master's degree in North African and Middle Eastern studies, started many of these ministries with me, with almost no offices, no budgets, and a very low salary, simply because she believed in the mission. And there's Viola, who has worked in her spare time to advocate, educate, and be a voice of the voiceless. I also think of Nuha, who spent fifteen years in the United States, finishing two master's degrees and a earning a doctorate from the University of Michigan, Ann Arbor. After months of discussions, Nuha decided to leave Ann Arbor and join our team because she believed that she is most needed here and now. And I think of Carol, who finished her master's degree in Brussels in November 2001 while Bethlehem was experiencing almost daily shelling from the F-16s and Apache helicopters. She wrote me from Brussels, saying that she wanted to come back to Bethlehem and that if we had a place for her, she would love to join our team. I thought she must be crazy to want to come back then, but we hired her because only people who are so committed can make a difference. I think of our other Carol, who after going through a terrible experience during the Intifada, decided to emigrate to the United States. After a few months, she wrote to say she was coming back, since she couldn't stay away and watch TV from afar, away from her people. Then there are Faten, who delivered her daughter while Bethlehem was under curfew; Sami, who was used by soldiers as a human shield; Lara, who came under curfew to the center to ship crafts to buyers in the United States; and

Shadi, whose house was shot at by the Israeli military. It would take me a long time to tell the stories of all the others who are here because they do not want to be spectators but actors. It is through the commitment of them all that the center was able to grow from a one-man show into one of the largest private employers in the Bethlehem region.

Our staff members are here by choice. Some of them came back to Palestine because they wanted to make a difference. With the ongoing debate on the right of return for the Palestinian refugees, thousands of Palestinians want to do what our staff has done, but they cannot. In fact, this question needs to be addressed according to the respective United Nations resolutions and implemented in a creative way.

However, talking about the right is one thing, and preparing the ground for the Palestinian refugees to return is another. Israel is blocking any serious talks about the right of return, while our political leaders are just paying it lip service. While the Palestinian leadership praises the right of return with words, the policies on the ground forced many who were living in Palestine to leave. A lack of political stability and vision, the devastating and senseless militarization of the Intifada, and poor economic strategies forced many to emigrate, most of whom were the well-to-do or the well-educated, among them a good number of Palestinian Christians. This led many Palestinians to lose hope in their country and in its potential.

What has given our visitors from abroad hope was to see another trend here at the center. At a time when many were leaving, a minority here dared to stay and refused to leave. They have dedication and commitment to the community, which are quite different from nationalism. The staff members who decided to return were not guided by blind ideology or rigid patriotism. Rather, they were guided by a simple faith that their place is not where life is easiest, but where their services are most needed.

Besides our staff's commitment, the second source of hope our visitors mention is our persistence in doing ministry and expanding it, even under the most challenging conditions. Three of the main projects, which we started months before the millennium celebrations, were unfinished when the Intifada began. The first is Dar al-Kalima School, an innovative educational institution from kindergarten through high school, which opened on September 3, 2000, only three and a half weeks before the Intifada. Now 240 children are enrolled in this new school. This school was actually never officially dedicated. Three attempts to do so failed because of the escalating conflict.

In March 2002 and without any reason, the Israeli army invaded the school, jailed the guard, and vandalized many doors, windows, and walls. The moment the Israeli troops left the school, we documented the devastation and then immediately got busy repairing the damage and replacing destroyed doors and windows. If others have a desire to destroy, we have a commitment to build, to restore the shattered beauty, and to educate our future generations.

The second unfinished project is our cultural and conference center, which stood as a skeleton when the Intifada started. The many closures and curfews caused work delays totaling almost two years. Moreover, Israeli troops stormed the center on April 2, 2002, leaving extensive destruction behind. Yet whenever the curfew was lifted, even if only for a few hours or a week, workers came to build. When the center's furniture arrived from the port on a curfew day, it was unloaded from the trucks into the center by a group of American Mennonites. At times, when Israel was implementing a policy of determined destruction, we were busy with creative construction. We didn't give up for a minute wanting to have a state-of-the-art cultural and conference center that is meant to be a place of a worldwide encounter. This has been happening during a time when Israel has sought to destroy what we built and to put up walls around us, isolating us from the world. Nevertheless, this will not deter us from our mission of building bridges. We choose to respond to the culture of violence with the power of culture. Our conference and cultural center became a unique facility not only in Bethlehem but throughout Palestine. A $5 million project that was funded by the Ministry of Foreign Affairs of Finland as their contribution to the millennium celebration was finally and after much delay inaugurated on September 1, 2003. In the first six months of its operation it hosted over 12,000 visitors, who came to enjoy concerts, watch movies, listen to debates, and participate in public workshops.

Our third big project is the Dar al-Kalima Health and Wellness Center. This project was built almost entirely during the Intifada. It was not at all easy to get the cement, iron bars, and tiles for the project. The whole endeavor was tiring. Yet we continued to work, knowing that the health and wellness of our people were at stake and that hope and healing were never so crucial as at this time. Now patients are coming to the center from as far as Tulkarem in the northwestern part of the West Bank, sometimes crossing eight checkpoints and spending hours on the way, just to get the treatment they need.

Whenever I've given a delegation a tour of all of these facilities, the people have become speechless. These buildings speak a different language. We don't want to show our visitors only the destruction done to our facilities and country; we also want to show them all the great things happening under the most difficult circumstances. After such a tour, visitors who arrived feeling depressed from what they had seen happening in our country leave with a new sense of hope. Here they've seen the potential of Palestine if there is a vision, faith, the will, and the right management of human and financial resources.

As Palestinians, we're used to telling only the story of our suffering. However, the story of our successes and hopes needs to be told as well. It's not good simply to depress our friends day and night, for we all need moments of being uplifted and charged with new strength. We've been conditioning ourselves to run a hundred yards, but we are in fact in a marathon. Our struggle is neither easy nor short, and we have to condition ourselves for the long challenge ahead. We need moments of joy and hope in the midst of all of this hopelessness. Otherwise, we won't be able to continue our journey.

Some visitors haven't liked what they've seen here. They wanted to see us as mere victims, hopeless and helpless. But that attitude victimizes us, the victims. Although we are victims, we are not *only* victims. We have fears and tears, but we have hopes and dreams, too. We work hard on both fears and dreams. We aren't just helpless people, nor are we a hopeless case. Rather, we can make a difference in our lives and in the lives of those around us.

It's important for us to hear our visitors tell us that what they've seen here has given them hope, strength, and commitment to go back and make a change. That's why, when we tell the story of our center as a beacon of hope, we must mention our partners. So let me tell you about Sandra, who, before the Intifada, lived in Jerusalem. After it began and while Bethlehem was experiencing daily shelling, Sandra decided to move here to Bethlehem to be with us and share our fears and hopes with the rest of the world through e-mail. Then there's Andreas, who decided to stay and continue teaching our tour-guiding students, preparing them to be ambassadors for their country. Next, there is Johannes, who refused to be evacuated from Bethlehem. He stayed to continue giving music classes so that our kids would not surrender to the noises of shelling and bombing and forget to play beautiful melodies. Hundreds of others have been called to be our partners but not necessarily among us.

These are what I call the "wise people from the West." They followed the star leading them to Bethlehem and brought with them all kinds of gifts. Among them are Rich, who used all his connections to find new friends for our work; Gregg, who brought with him a great financial commitment for our ministry; and Ruth, who kept sending letters to her senators and representatives in Congress, asking them to do something about our plight.

If I were to mention all those involved in our friendship associations and our partners—individuals, churches, governmental and nongovernmental organizations—that believed in what we were doing and wanted to make a difference, I would fill pages. All of them, Palestinians and internationals, have been perplexed but not in despair (2 Corinthians 4:8), working for nothing less than a brighter Bethlehem, making room for hope.

15

A Christmas Gift to Bethlehem

At Christmas Lutheran Church in Bethlehem is an old pipe organ with a unique history. Made in Germany 110 years ago, the organ traveled by ship in 1893 to Jaffa, a small port on the Mediterranean that was then part of the great Ottoman Empire. In service for more than a century, the pipe organ survived two World Wars and more than ten regional wars. In 1967 an Israeli bomb fell near it. In 1987 Israeli soldiers were firing within a few feet of it. And in 2002 Israeli tanks stood just outside of the sanctuary that houses it.

This organ saw the Ottomans ruling Bethlehem, then the British, the Jordanians, and the Israelis, as well as the Palestinian Authority. Most of these ruling authorities have come and gone, but the organ has remained faithful, standing in its place in the balcony. It has been played during baptismal services, weddings, and funerals. It was always in solidarity with the Palestinian Christian community at Christmas Lutheran Church—like a faithful spouse, in good times and bad, in sickness and in health, for richer and for poorer.

Yet, in 1993, when the sanctuary celebrated its hundredth anniversary, the pipe organ was sent into retirement. It was kept in the church balcony but was not used in the service anymore. Much of it had deteriorated through lack of regular maintenance, and many parts were irreparably damaged. It was clear the instrument would not live to the end of the twentieth century.

Then, in 1997, a Lutheran pastor from Minnesota, Arden Haug, visited Christmas Lutheran and asked to play our organ. I told him it hadn't been functioning for several years. He asked if we were interested in restoring it. I answered, "Yes, but rebuilding is very costly, and there's no way a small congregation like ours can do it. That's why it's not on our priority list. We have more pressing needs. But if you know of a way to do it, we'll be very thankful, since this organ is one of the oldest in the Holy Land and an important part of Bethlehem's heritage."

I added that it would be great to finish this task before the millennium celebrations, since we were expecting millions of Christian pilgrims and hundreds of choirs to visit the Holy Land near the end of 1999 and throughout 2000. It would be marvelous if they could use this sanctuary with a restored pipe organ for concerts, celebrations, and services.

Pastor Haug said he'd try his best, once back in the United States. I must admit that I soon forgot my conversation with him. So many pilgrims and tourists visit the Holy Land, develop wild ideas, and then, once back in their home countries, get caught up in their daily business and forget about their Holy Land visions. This pattern, however, was not true for that pastor from Minnesota. He was dedicated to this mission. Back in the United States, he contacted Lutheran friends and a Minnesota organ builder to see if they were interested in working with him on this project.

One year later, I was astonished to receive a letter from the organ builder, asking many questions about this old instrument. In May 1998, the organ builder, Roland Rutz, visited Bethlehem to assess the organ situation. At that time, Bethlehem was one huge construction site. The Old City was undergoing a total renovation of its infrastructure, facades, and tourist services. For Bethlehem 2000, the Palestinian Authority invested over $200 million in the city's infrastructure. Rebuilding the old organ seemed to fit this endeavor perfectly. The future of the little town of Bethlehem seemed never as promising as during these days. Bethlehem was preparing itself for a new millennium, and we thought it was natural to rebuild a nineteenth-century organ for the twenty-first century.

But for such an overhaul, the organ had to be shipped to the organ builder's studio in Morristown, Minnesota. For me, this was cause for a headache. All seaports and airports were controlled exclusively by Israel. All imports into and exports out of the West Bank went through Israeli hands. The organ had to go through checkpoints and would most likely be stopped and searched. If the instrument left us, we weren't sure the Israelis would let it come back. Even if they did, might they try to tax it as if it were new?

Nevertheless, we decided to go ahead and ship the organ to the United States. But before doing so, we had to raise the necessary funds. The projection was that this endeavor would cost some $130,000. Not a cent of this amount was yet available. Pastor Haug approached our partner Lutheran church in Minneapolis, Christ the Redeemer, to see if people there would be willing to lead such a major funding effort. They agreed to do so.

By June 1999, Christ the Redeemer was ready to launch its campaign. Raising the needed amount required a year and a half of hard work. Some ten thousand brochures were distributed, over five thousand individual mailings were sent to individuals and congregations, and hundreds of personal appearances were made. Gifts came from all across the United States, totaling $135,000, enough to pay for complete rebuilding of the organ and for its two trips across the ocean, plus taxes and fees to Israel's port officials. In all, more than five hundred individuals donated, and almost one hundred gifts came from congregations and other institutions. A highlight of the fund-raising occurred on Reformation Sunday 2000, when a special benefit recital was held at St. Stephen Lutheran Church in suburban Minneapolis. I was able to be present and deliver thanks from people in Bethlehem.

Roland Rutz came to Bethlehem in February 2000 and spent a week dismantling and packing the organ, getting it ready for shipment to Minnesota. The organ left from the port in Haifa on March 22. (The Jaffa port, where the ship that originally brought the organ had docked in the late nineteenth century, was no longer in use as an international port; Haifa has developed into the main seaport in Israel today.)

The ship carrying our organ sailed through the Mediterranean and across the Atlantic, arriving at

Boston in May. From Boston, the organ was trucked to Minnesota. An instrument that had been originally manufactured in Germany and had lived its entire life in Bethlehem was now for five months undergoing major repair in the United States. Roland Rutz had prepared a schedule that would have the organ ready to be delivered to Bethlehem in time for the millennium celebrations. The target date was Christmas Eve 2000, and the 150-voice Alumni Choir of Wartburg College of Waverly, Iowa, was scheduled to give a concert at Christmas Lutheran Church to celebrate the organ's rededication.

Yet in the Holy Land, events are never predictable. We can develop the best plans, only to see that political realities on the ground will alter those plans. One day, the situation might look very promising, and the next day, chaos can erupt. That was the case with the schedule for our organ. All plans for the rededication of the organ were in place. Great millennium celebrations were under way. But while the organ was getting its final touches, the second Intifada started on September 28, 2000, as a reaction to the demonstrative and provocative visit to the al-Aqsa Mosque in Jerusalem by Ariel Sharon, then opposition leader in Israel. Within a few days, the political climate had changed 180 degrees. Before, there had been optimism that peace was in sight; a political agreement seemed to be at hand between the two political leaders (Yasir Arafat for the Palestinians and Ehud Barak for the Israelis), under the guidance of U.S. president Bill Clinton. The hope disappeared suddenly, leaving nothing behind but escalating violence.

In the Middle East, things can be very deceiving, since no one knows when winds will change their directions. All of the optimism with which Bethlehem had been preparing for the millennium celebrations was gone. When the organ arrived in Haifa on December 15, 2000, it must have felt that it had arrived in a different country than the one it had left nine months earlier.

Bethlehem was by then under strict siege, experiencing daily shelling by F-16 fighters and Apache helicopters. Not only did the Wartburg Alumni Choir cancel its planned trip to the Holy Land, so also did thousands of tourists. And the organ? For six days it was stuck at Haifa's port. Israel was refusing to process any goods headed for the West Bank. Only after days of negotiations and the payment of more taxes and fees was the organ released from the port on December 21. It arrived in Bethlehem late that afternoon.

Only a few days were left to reinstall the pipe organ in time for worship at 5:00 PM on Christmas Eve. Roland Rutz and two of his assistants assured me they would work nonstop to have the organ ready for that rededication service. For most of three days, they worked around the clock to finish the task. In the early afternoon on December 24, the goal seemed within reach.

Then came another unexpected occurrence. Around 3:30 the organ's power supply died. A German-made power transformer blew up just ninety minutes before the service was set to start. The momentum was lost. Everyone felt deeply disappointed. When Rutz brought me this news, I couldn't believe what I was hearing. After all this hard work by so many people and within reach of our goal, this had to happen! I asked him if there was anything we could do.

He replied, "Can I use your car battery?"

"For sure," I said. I went outside, removed the battery from my car, and took it to him in the organ loft.

"I've never heard of it being done on this type of electric action, but your battery might be our last resort," Rutz said. He took the battery and connected it to the organ. At 4:50, ten minutes before the service was to start, the organ was playing again. Hallelujah! It worked!

Our joy at hearing music from the magnificent nineteenth-century instrument, now revitalized for the twenty-first, with power provided by a car battery, was overwhelming. In the meantime, the church filled with people.

I opened the service with the following words:

Welcome to this Christmas Eve service 2000 at Christmas Lutheran, here in Bethlehem. This is a very special Christmas for us. Bethlehem is sealed off, yet we have here partners from the United States and from Germany, who came to be with us as a sign of their solidarity and friendship.

This is indeed a special Christmas, because tonight we are dedicating our rebuilt organ. This organ has an amazing history, with over thirty thousand miles in its account. Built in Berlin in 1892, it was brought to Bethlehem and has been used in this church during most of the twentieth century. However, it began to age, and people thought it was going to die and be buried in Palestine. But through the vision, dedication, and generous support, especially of our partner congregation, Lutheran Church of Christ the Redeemer in Minneapolis, the organ was brought to Minnesota, restored by the Rutz Organ Company, and arrived in Haifa last Sunday and in Bethlehem on Thursday.

My special thanks tonight to Roland Rutz and his crew, who worked very hard for the last ten months and even harder for the last forty-eight hours to have it ready for this worship. Ms. Karen Ullestad came all the way from Iowa to play the first tunes on this old organ. Our organist, George Abu Dayyah, is speechless, seeing a dream come true.

Tonight we are dedicating this organ for a mission impossible. At a time when the little town of Bethlehem is getting used to the sounds of gunfire, shelling, and bombing, this organ is restored so that our children may hear new sounds—sounds of justice, songs of peace, and tunes of compassion. At a time when Palestine is still suffering from occupation, this organ will play new melodies—melodies of freedom and liberation. Freedom from sin, freedom from decadence, freedom to love even your enemy. And in the midst of suffering, we are rejoicing today and singing:

O little town of Bethlehem, the organs still do play,
Of Jesus in a manger and angels on the way.
Our music and our singing is louder than a gun.
And church bells in their ringing remind us we
    have won.

    —verse written for the occasion by the Reverend Herb Brokering, Lutheran pastor and poet in Minnesota

16

Samar

Samar, a thirty-eight-year-old Palestinian Christian woman, never finished high school. She lost her father when she was thirteen but was lucky to have married George, a young Lutheran man from the same village. Samar and George were blessed with two wonderful children. Life wasn't easy for them, but they were together as they struggled to survive. Their daily concern was how to pay their rent at the end of each month, how to pay the water and electricity bills, and how to secure the necessary food and clothing for their children.

In September 2000, their situation was somewhat stable. Samar was working in a newly opened Christian guesthouse, and George worked in a textile factory in a neighboring town. George was starting to dream of a better future. He approached me to ask for a small loan to buy a few sewing machines so that he could open a small workshop at home and work there, especially as the wages in his industry were very low. Although he worked eight hours a day, six days a week, he earned less than $400 per month, and he was seldom paid on time. I encouraged him to develop his idea of a home business and asked him to work on a business plan and bring it to me for further discussion. Samar and George were just barely managing. They were looking for a better future, at least for their kids. At the same time, I didn't want him to take a loan without knowing the risks of such a step. The following weeks showed how unpredictable the situation was.

When the Intifada started and Israel responded with its collective punishment and military strikes and invasions, the situation got worse and worse for Samar and George. The guesthouse where Samar was working had to close. Tourists no longer were interested in coming to Bethlehem, or even Israel. The textile factory in which George worked also had to close. The Palestinian textile companies had been working as subcontractors supplying bigger Israeli textile companies, since wages in the West Bank were much lower than those in Israel. After the Intifada, Israeli companies were no longer interested in working with Palestinian subcontractors. At the same time, the Israeli companies discovered that wages in Jordan were even lower than in the West Bank. With American subsidies, the companies moved the whole textile industry to Jordan. After more than fifteen years of work for the same company, George lost his job. The owner of the company gathered all the workers, explained the situation to them, and told them that he was bankrupt and that they would receive only part of their compensation, even with some delays. Eventually, George received four checks totaling around $1,000 as his severance pay for over fifteen years of work.

For Samar and George, this was the end of all of their dreams. They both were unemployed, without any income whatsoever. During the first few months, they were able to live on the compensation George had received from his company. They hoped that the situation would soon become normal so they would be able to work again. What they didn't expect was that this situation would continue for weeks, then months, and even for years.

Samar and George, members of Christmas Lutheran Church, were put on the congregation's social payroll and became dependent on food supplies from other social institutions of the Bethlehem region. Of course, this wasn't an arrangement they liked or the congregation could afford for long. We had to find alternatives so that Samar and George could, like Adam and Eve, "eat bread" by "the sweat of their face" (Genesis 3:19). Our philosophy is not to give people in need fish, but to teach them how to fish so that they can live in dignity. But how could they earn a living in a city where the unemployment rate had reached almost 75 percent? Thousands of Palestinians who were better educated, were much more skilled, and had many contacts were searching for jobs as well.

Samar was gifted with an artistic touch. She was one of the first students at our arts and crafts center. In 1998 she took the center's first course in stained glass, led by Corinne Whitlach, director of Churches for Middle East Peace, based in Washington, D.C. Corinne's idea was to produce small stained-glass art pieces out of broken bottles and glass. This was the method she taught her students, and she insisted that they should not buy new glass for their production but rather use old glass as a form of recycling. Samar was one of Corinne's best students.

Several years have now passed since Samar took this course. When I met with her in 2001, she wasn't very motivated to produce stained-glass works. I could certainly understand her point of view. How could she produce stained-glass art pieces in such a context? Who in the Palestinian community could afford to buy such items when people were mostly concerned about their daily bread? The other important target market for these items was tourists, and they weren't coming to our town.

Even so, I encouraged Samar to participate in a course we were offering during the Intifada: glass fusing. It is a technique in which several layers of glass are melted together. The bottom layer provides a base, and the other layers give coloring and texture. Wonderful scenes, animals, flowers, and other images can be produced to make ornaments for hanging on windows and walls. This course was funded by NORAD, the Norwegian Agency for Development Cooperation, with the idea of using broken glass to produce art pieces. Samar took part in this training course as well. At least it gave her something to look forward to doing every day.

As part of the project, we developed a Web site (www.bethlehemchristmasmarket.org) to market the items produced by the artists so that they have a source of income. We thought that if the tourists could not come to Palestine, then Palestine would have to reach out to tourists. The artists received a few orders via the Internet, and they were able to organize a beautiful bazaar for Christmas 2001 at our center. They were looking forward to a new course that would be offered in a third technique, known as glass beading.

In 2002 these art courses proved to be much more important than we had anticipated. During the Israeli invasion, tank shelling, and air strikes on Bethlehem in April of that year, hundreds of windows were shattered, and broken glass became the symbol of our town's destruction. More importantly, the broken glass symbolized the broken hopes and shattered dreams of so many people. Creatively using this broken glass matched one of the roles we see for our center: shaping new symbols for a new reality, transforming the symbols of destruction and war into symbols of hope and peace.

Samar was already starting to produce little angels of stained glass. In autumn 2002, the Christian Council of Norway ordered a large quantity of such stained-glass angels. The order was so large that Samar couldn't produce them alone. So one day, Samar surprised us by bringing George to our arts and crafts workshops. She asked him to sit there, watch her, and get a sense of how she created the angels. She tutored him as he produced his first pieces. Samar's husband became her student, and she his supervisor. What a revolution in the Middle Eastern context!

Our Christmas 2002 newsletter highlighted these angels:

Dear sisters and brothers,

Hundreds of angels were seen during this Advent season in many congregations throughout Norway. People said those angels have a head, a body, and two wings. They were even able to touch them. Those angels were made out of glass, fragments of broken bottles thrown away or glass destroyed during the Israeli invasion of Bethlehem. Human hands picked the glass fragments from among the rubble, then they were assembled together by some of the poorest of the poor in the Bethlehem region at our art workshops. Ordered by the Christian Council of Norway to be sent to hundreds of congregations, those angels told all about "the hopes and fears of all the years" that people have in Bethlehem today. The broken glass pieces are a sign of the brokenness of our world, and it is also the reason for God to incarnate. Through His incarnation he brought the divine and the human back together, He picked what seems to be worthless and hopeless and transformed it into a beautiful and whole creation. It is this incarnation, which took place here in Bethlehem two thousand years ago, which gives us the strength to continue to look for broken lives and hopes and to transform them through art into angels, messengers of justice, peace, and dignity. We would like to thank you for being our partners in this "mission impossible." With God's Spirit and your support and dedication, you made this mission possible.

These angels made my Christmas 2002 joyful. On December 25, as we were celebrating the Eucharist at Christmas Lutheran Church, I stood holding the bread and watching Samar and George walk forward to receive Holy Communion. Samar wore a beautiful new dress, and George had on a brand-new suit. As they came closer, I felt how proud they were. For the first

time in over two years, they were not on the social payroll of the congregation. For the first time since the start
of the Intifada, they were employed. They were proud
of having bought their clothes with money they had
earned themselves. I could feel their sense of dignity
from being self-supporting.

When they stood before me to take the bread, tears
were in my eyes. I was so proud of them. Not only had
they made it economically, but they had also become
ambassadors for Palestine. The angels they have produced tell the story of shattered hopes restored,
destroyed dreams transformed, and broken lives made
new, unique, artistic, and whole.

17

Christmas and the Wall

For he is our peace; in his flesh he has made both groups into one and has broken down the dividing wall, that is, the hostility between us.

—Ephesians 2:14

For Christmas Eve 2003, I decided to preach on this verse from Paul's letter to the Ephesians. The reading must have sounded a little strange. It's a passage sometimes used for Good Friday, rather than Christmas Eve. I chose it because I believe that it refers to both the incarnation and crucifixion. They belong together anyhow. But for many, Paul's words might not sound too Christmassy.

The passage does talk about peace, and Christmas has become the feast of "a sort of peace" that no one can really fully describe. In fact, the usual emphasis is kind of a "cheap peace"—something to preach about when one is not well prepared or a bit of wishful thinking when one is not ready to do much. Personally, I am bored with all of this talk about peace around Christmastime. Christmas has become a season for joyful peace talkers rather than blessed peacemakers.

In our Palestinian context, "peace talk" is often a recipe for managing the conflict rather than resolving it. It is as if there were an un-gentlemen's agreement: the world continues to talk peace while Israel continues to build the wall. And while Christians all over the world sing "O Little Town of Bethlehem," Israel makes sure that this town stays as little as possible, as little as two square miles, surrounded with thirty-mile-long walls, fences, and trenches with no future expansion possibilities whatsoever.

I preached my Christmas Eve sermon to people facing this reality. At Christmas we don't need to ignore this reality, forget it or beautify it, but we have to face it, as we do every day. We know what it means to tens of thousands of our people, how it cuts them off from their fields, medical services, and schools. We're worried about our children and future generations, who will grow up seeing nothing around them but high concrete walls, ugly trenches, and security fences. We're worried that they might eventually live with walls in their minds, forgetting that the sky is the limit.

As Christians we dare to speak out, not to demonize the other, but because we believe there is an alternative. Christians have to take Christmas in Bethlehem seriously, because on that holy night and in this very place, God chose to be very concrete, to take flesh, and to take our world very seriously. We Christians are unafraid to face the brutal reality around us because we believe in a power mightier than walls and put our faith in a peace that exceeds all human understanding.

On that recent Christmas Eve, I reminded my congregation that no one understood the true meaning of peace better than St. Paul. Originally named Saul, this former Jewish leader, zealot, persecutor, and hard-liner committed himself to making sure that a wall of separation was built and kept between his community and its enemies. He was ready to attack, terrorize, and even sanction the killing of whoever dared to question the importance of this wall for the security of his community. He did that in the stoning of St. Stephen, the first Christian martyr, and he did it to many others as well. For Saul there was no compromise. For Saul the ideological wall of separation was necessary to preserve his people's identity, demography, and security. This was the way he had been brought up. This was what he had been taught.

However, this same radical person was radically transformed. On the road to Damascus, Saul had a unique encounter with no one less than Jesus of Nazareth, God incarnate. This encounter made Saul discover what true peacemaking is all about, and he described it as breaking down dividing walls of hostility (Ephesians 2:14). From that moment, the zealot Saul became the passionate apostle Paul. His great discovery was that God in Christ broke the walls of hostility between the human and the divine. The wall of sin was brought down by God, and in its place a bridge of amazing grace was constructed.

For Paul this discovery had only one conclusion: If God in Christ has destroyed the wall of hostility between the divine and the human, then there is no place for walls between peoples, tribes, cultures, and nations. The incarnation—the reason we Christians gather on Christmas Eve—was thus nothing sentimental but a radical transformation. This very reality of the incarnation was mightier than Saul's old convictions. It was so powerful that it transformed the ancient world and created a new reality.

On Christmas Eve, I proclaimed that the same far-reaching message of Christmas is still transforming people all around the world. I shared with my congregation the story of Judy, who for over twenty years has been living as a mission coworker in the Congo. She recently wrote a letter to her bishop in England, saying,

> Each Christmas I am challenged more and more to see the power of this time; what Jesus came to do; and I find the tinsel, the soppy carols an affront to the true message. When I received photos of the total destruction of my house in Bunia with just the walls and roof standing and our pastor looking at the papers everywhere, I realized what is the meaning of Christmas. Jesus came down to sort out this mess, to bring a way out of the useless destruction. Praise Him, but may we take up the "war-cry" and stand for Him to bring others the way of salvation.

At a time when a wall of hostility was being built around our town, the message from Paul that I read for Christmas 2003 encouraged my congregation and me. We recommitted ourselves to breaking down all walls of hatred and hostilities, be they concrete walls or ideological, racial, political, social, and economic ones. From the hometown of Christ, we have no other message on the day when we celebrate his life: "For he is our peace; in his flesh he has made both groups into one and has broken down the dividing wall, that is, the hostility between us." We wish ourselves nothing less than for the transforming power of the incarnation to strengthen all of us in our commitment to breaking down walls, making peace, and building bridges.

18

Building Walls or Planting Olive Trees?

While I was writing this book, a friend asked me, "How can you write of hope when settlements are expanding throughout the West Bank like mushrooms and a twenty-six-foot-high wall is being built around almost every city in the West Bank, transforming Palestinian towns into big prisons?" My friend told me that writing about hope makes no sense when our community is being strangled from all sides. He insisted that fear, war, and conflict are the bitter realities of our world. Considering these realities, said my friend, writing about hope must be a way to escape the bitterness of this world and instead cling to a utopia. He asked, "Are you so depressed by the current situation that you just want to hear something hopeful so you feel better?"

I can understand why my friend was concerned about my sanity. Usually, we write about hope when we're expecting something good to happen, even if the possibility of its happening is minimal. How can we hope in times of despair, when there seems to be no future to hope for? Not much progress is expected for justice, for peace, for better times. It seems crazy to hold on to hope when the dream seems to be shattered—simply and finally lost.

Our recent history as Palestinians is a story of violence, misery, and oppression: thirty-six years of Israeli occupation, four years of uprising from 1987 to 1991, the Gulf War in 1991. During these years, we often were under house arrest because of curfews imposed on our cities. Many young Palestinians were shot, wounded, and killed. Others, including church members, were arrested and imprisoned.

In spite of all that, we had hope. We continued to hope that one day justice would prevail. We had a vision that, one day, Israelis and Palestinians would be able to live together in peace. A vision that occupation would one day end and that Israelis and Palestinians would discover the human side of the other. The peace process in 1993 was an expression of this hope and of this vision.

However, during the last few years, since 2002, this hope has evaporated almost completely. Israeli tanks surrounded Palestinian towns and villages. Over two million of our people were put under house arrest for months. Apache helicopters were used to fire on Palestinian neighborhoods. Many West Bank cities have been filled with the sounds of missiles and tanks bombing neighborhoods, as well as the screams of little children scared to death. Israeli tanks and munitions destroyed much of what we had built for the millennium celebrations around our church in Bethlehem. Not only were all the projects and buildings that we started in the last twelve years suddenly at risk, but our very lives and those of our members, friends, and children were endangered.

The first victim of these last years was hope. Hope was assassinated. Our vision of peace became unrealistic, justice was impossible, coexistence nothing but a myth. The crisis in Palestine today is this: The majority of Palestinians and the majority of Israelis have lost their hopes and visions.

In the last two years, Palestinian children lost their ability to dream. Now they have only nightmares. Youth and adults feel there is no longer anything to hope for. They have nothing to long for, nothing to dream about. The suicide bombings are an expression of this hopelessness. People believe in a life after death, true, but they find no life *before* death that is worth living here and now! This is the crisis: Suicide bombers do not see the potential of their place here, nor do they have a vision left for tomorrow.

The current crisis in Israel/Palestine arises from a leadership lacking vision. Israeli Prime Minister Ariel Sharon has no vision whatsoever for peace. His only vision is that of the old apartheid of South Africa. The Palestine Liberation Organization's only vision was that of liberating Palestine, rather than building it stone by stone. The PLO therefore could not transform itself from a liberation organization into an organ of a democratic, innovative, and creative state.

The international community, too, lacks vision. In the last thirty-some years of occupation, the international community could not develop a vision of hope for the region. Its role was basically to "manage the conflict," to keep the status quo of occupation, and to help contain serious escalation. And the Bush administration chose not to interfere in the latest Israeli-Palestinian conflict. They gave up on it. At least it has not been one of the priorities on their agenda.

The United Nations supported the Palestinians with many resolutions but failed to implement any of them. When U.S. Secretary of State Colin Powell addressed the U.N. Security Council on February 6, 2003, regarding Iraq, he concluded by saying, "My colleagues, we have an obligation to our citizens; we have an obligation to this body to see that our resolutions are complied with." We wonder how the same countries and the same council have been dealing with their obligation toward the Palestinian people. We would like to see Secretary Powell present satellite pictures of the illegal yet expanding Israeli colonies in the West Bank and Gaza. We ask ourselves why the same country and the same council are tolerating Israel's total failure to comply with the U.N.'s many resolutions in regard to the Israeli-Palestinian conflict.

A hopeful vision cannot be mere words, statements, or resolutions. In fact, people gave up hope because there was a clear discrepancy between what they were seeing and what they were hearing. They were hearing the false prophets say, "Peace . . . peace," but on the ground there was no peace. They were hearing visions of a new, prosperous Middle East, but they were seeing nothing but the old Middle East. And the peace process proved to be more process than peace.

The real challenge today for Palestinians in general, and for Christian Palestinians in particular, is this: How can we hope in a context of despair and hold on to our vision in times of bitter conflict and war? This is so important, for, as the Bible says, without a vision, the people perish.

Yet if the objective situation offers little reasonable expectation of improvement, what then is the character of hope? It's not, anymore, a wish that tomorrow will be better. It's not an expectation of progress. We don't see a light at the end of the tunnel. Hope doesn't mean that things are in any way improving or that all we have to do is to sit back, wait, and watch. Waiting, being passive, and feeling optimistic about the future—these are false hope. True hope is active: it is all about developing a strategy for action, for work, for getting engaged and involved.

True hope is a powerful and critical concept for those living amid conflict. There is a great need to redefine and reclaim hope, especially among the oppressed. Hope and vision are powerful if they are owned and lived by the oppressed. Hope is rewarding because it offers a real alternative. It opens a window of great opportunities, and it sets free the creativity of the oppressed.

Suffering people desperately need to transform their feelings of being overwhelmed by the extent of the suffering into an ability to take control of the suffering by developing a vision for the future. When you have hope, you resist becoming data to be gathered or a case study on human rights violations—someone to pity or something to observe. Rightly understood, hope is nothing less than gaining control over one's own destiny. The vicious cycle of conflict is often so powerful that the oppressed become double victims—victims of the oppressors and also victims of their own actions and reactions, which harm them much more than they harm their oppressors. Hope teaches the oppressed to stop being merely victims (even with a just cause) who do not know how to achieve goals and dreams.

Hope is the strength to dare to break this vicious cycle. It is the art of interrupting the established pattern of events—not out of weakness but out of strength, out of one's own will, at one's own time, and in response to one's own decision. To hold hope is to resist heightening the potential for self- and mutual destruction. In that sense, holding to a hopeful vision is an act to save the "soul" of one's nation and group.

To hope is to move from being interested in earning the solidarity of the world and into a state of empowerment, where one starts planning and strategizing. Hope does not lead us to stop resisting but rather moves us to start reflecting on how to resist effectively. Resistance is no longer an end in itself but rather a plan within a well-thought-out strategy.

Hope is important for the Israelis, too. They have to see how they can gain control of their lives, for their own sake and that of their children. They must find a way to stop the ambitions of their military government and start expressing the policy they want implemented in their name. They have to overcome their fears as we overcome our fears.

Hope is of utmost importance to both Israelis and Palestinians. Hope gives all of us the ability to rethink our own story and history and at the same time to challenge that of the "enemy." It is the art of seeing things from a different angle, from a different perspective and not just from one's own narrow perspective. Unless we can put ourselves in the shoes of the other, we will never understand how the chain reaction is set off. Israelis and Palestinians have proved that they can make their own lives and that of their enemies very bitter. They have made the point that they can destroy each other.

What Israelis and Palestinians need is a vision of how to live together. The vision for Israel and Palestine is to realize the paradox that it does not benefit a country if it wins the support of whole world and loses its neighbor. What is the benefit if Israel wins the moral and financial support of the American Jewish community and the Christian right yet loses its Palestinian neighbors? What is the benefit if the Palestinians win the sympathy and support of most of the Arab and Islamic countries and lose their Israeli neighbors? Those supporters pay dollars but make us pay with blood.

A hopeful vision is also important for American and European Christians. Not because they need to be pro-Palestinian, but because they need to stop being spectators in their own country. We are not asking for more statements on the Middle East. We are asking for action—not only for our sake, but also for their own sake and that of their respective countries. Citizens of these countries must care that their money be spent not to subsidize the Israeli occupation but to create a just peace in the region.

My hope for all of us is very simple. I'm not asking for the moon or the stars. I'm asking that we be involved together—Palestinians, Israelis, Americans, and Europeans—to stop being spectators and to become actors. Together we can make a difference.

What does this mean for me today? My captor daily seeks to make life harder for me. He encircles my people with barbed wire; he builds walls around us, and his army sets many boundaries around us. He succeeds in keeping thousands of us in camps and prisons. Yet despite all these efforts, he has not succeeded in taking my hope or vision from me. He could not imprison them. His suppression could not keep me from thinking of a joint future with him. His brutality did not succeed in discouraging me from dreaming of a peaceful coexistence with him.

What does true hope imply for us as Palestinians? They make our life bitter so that our "brain" will "drain"; we create new opportunities for our young people to come and participate. They destroy our windows; we gather the glass pieces and transform them into pieces of art. They close our schools; we develop distance learning projects. They want to silence our story; we create ways to give a voice and a face to the voiceless. They build walls around our cities; we create electronic communication networks. They build settlements; we keep resisting such an apartheid system.

As Christians we should no longer be spectators in this world. We are actors on Christ's behalf. Sometimes we feel that the world in which we live has become a hell, depressing, with no progress, but our faith is in Christ, who is life. Hell is already overcome. Our call is not to transform this hell into a paradise but to transfer this hell into a world in which life is possible again.

Christian hope holds firm that it's never too late for faith in action and for acts of compassion. Christian hope does not surrender to the forces of death and despair but challenges them. Christian hope is to call upon those in the dark tunnel, in the valleys of death, to "come forth," as did Lazarus from the tomb, because here is someone who is the resurrection and the life. Hope is the best strategy to combat suicide bombers.

Holding to a hopeful vision in the context of war gives hope a new meaning. It is no longer something we see but rather something we practice, something we live, something we advocate, something we plant. At times when we feel as if the world must be coming to an end tomorrow, our call is not to wait, not to cry, nor to surrender. Rather, our only hopeful vision is to go out today into our garden, into our society, and plant olive trees. If we don't plant any trees today, there will be nothing tomorrow. But if we plant a tree today, there will be shade for the children to play in, there will be oil to heal the wounds, and there will be olive branches to wave when peace arrives.

Mitri Raheb is a Palestinian Arab and Christian pastor who ministers to his people in Bethlehem, where his family has lived for hundreds of years. Pastor of the Evangelical Lutheran Christmas Church in Bethlehem, he holds a doctorate from Marburg University in Germany. His first book, *I Am a Palestinian Christian* (Fortress Press, 1995), articulated a Palestinian theology. Raheb's efforts to bring home the plight of the Palestinian people have taken him around the world, and he is a frequent speaker in the United States. In 2003 the Luther Institute honored him with its Wittenberg Award for his service to the church, and the Holy Land Christian Ecumenical Foundation recognized him with its award for his commitment to assisting Christians in Palestine.

29071761R00096

Made in the USA
Lexington, KY
16 January 2014